You're just about to get the best PC you've ever owned

THERE'S NOTHING BETTER than the satisfaction you get from building your own PC, or upgrading your existing model. With computer prices cheaper than ever, it may seem a false economy, but look deeper and you'll see the true benefits.

For starters, when you build or upgrade your computer, you get to choose the components you want to use. In other words, you make sure you end up with the PC that fits your needs. It also means you can pick premium components, such as the ones we've recommended in this book, making your finished computer more stable and more reliable.

> " Our step-by-step workshops and advice will help you choose the right components at the right price "

The key advantage of building a PC yourself is that you can quickly take advantage of new technologies. In this book, for example, we've covered how to install and configure a solid state drive (SSD). Add one of these to your new build – or as an upgrade to your existing PC – and you can boost its performance, speeding up the time it takes to boot time and application loading times. Buy a computer off the shelf and you'll find that this kind of technology is reserved for only the most expensive computers.

What's more, building and upgrading your computer helps you learn how the insides of your PC work. Should you run into a problem later on, you'll be armed with the skill and knowledge to fix the problem yourself.

Our step-by-step workshops and advice will help you choose the right components at the right price. Happy building!

David Ludlow, Editor
david_ludlow@dennis.co.uk

Contents

From choosing the right kit to putting it all together and installing your software, our step-by-step guides will help you build the perfect PC

Chapter 1
ESSENTIALS

Find out what kit you'll need before you start building your PC, and learn some essential skills

PC builder's toolkit 6
Your workspace 8
Essential skills 10
Finding and installing drivers 12

Chapter 2
CHOOSING AN OPERATING SYSTEM

Find out how Microsoft's latest operating system compares to previous versions of Windows, as well as the free open-source alternative, Linux

Windows 7 16
Windows 7 editions 18
Linux 22

Chapter 3
CHOOSING YOUR HARDWARE

We explain what to look for when choosing the kit for your new build, and round up some of the best products available

Choosing your components 26
Budget and mid-range PCs 36
High-end and extreme PCs 37
Media centre and mini PCs 38
Essential peripherals 40

Chapter 4
BUILDING YOUR PC

Follow our step-by-step guides to creating the perfect PC

Taking the case apart 46
Installing the power supply 48
Installing the motherboard 50
Installing an Intel processor 56
Installing an AMD processor 57
Installing memory 58
Fitting the internal cables 60
Installing a hard disk 62
Installing an SSD 64
Installing an optical drive 66
Installing a graphics card 68
Installing expansion cards 72
Putting the case back together 75

Chapter 5
POWER ON

Take control of how your computer works

Into the BIOS 80

Chapter 6
INSTALLING AN OPERATING SYSTEM

Everything from configuration to installing drivers

How to install Windows 7 88
Improve Windows Media Center 92

Setting up an SSD 96
How to install Ubuntu Linux 100

Chapter 7
WINDOWS 7
Your complete guide to Microsoft's latest release

The desktop 106
Manage your windows 107
How to transfer your files 108
Keeping track of files 110
Sharing files with HomeGroup 112
How to perform an Anytime Upgrade 114

Chapter 8
NEW PC ESSENTIALS
Our pick of the best free software around

LibreOffice.org 3 118
AVG Anti-Virus Free Edition 119
Paint.NET 119
Picasa 3 120
CDBurnerXP 120
Free Download Manager 121
Freebyte Backup 121

7-Zip 121
VLC media player 121
Saving power with your new PC 122
Creating a backup 124
Adding virus protection 126

Chapter 9
TROUBLESHOOTING
Having problems? Don't panic – here are our tips and tricks to get your PC running smoothly

Boot problems 130
How to restore your system 135
Windows problems 136
Peripheral problems 144
Testing memory 150
Testing your hard disk 152
Testing your new PC for heat 154
Testing your processor 156

JARGON-BUSTER
Glossary 158
All the buzzwords and technology explained

44

64

CHAPTER 1
ESSENTIALS

BEFORE YOU RUSH out and buy the bits for your new computer, there are some essential things you need to know. In this chapter we'll show you what tools you'll require, the kind of workspace on which you should work, the skills you'll need and how to download the latest drivers for your new kit.

IN THIS CHAPTER

PC builder's toolkit   6

Your workspace   8

Essential skills   10

Finding and installing
    drivers   12

PC builder's

CAREFUL PREPARATION IS the key to every successful build, and the very first step is to get together the basic tools for the job. Over the next two pages, we'll show you how to put together a PC builder's toolkit that costs just a few pounds, but contains a range of hardware and software, which you can use again and again to tackle any build or future upgrade project with confidence.

WHAT YOU'LL GET WITH YOUR KIT

When you buy the components for your new PC, they will include a number of essential items. Your motherboard manual will have details of your motherboard's specifications and features, and an explanation of its ports and connectors. It'll also give you help with BIOS options and updates, and talk you through any bundled utility programs.

Your motherboard's box will contain all the data cables that you'll need to connect your hard disks and optical drives. There will be more cables than you need, so keep the other ones spare for future upgrades. Check the box carefully for any additional ports, such as rear-mounted USB, FireWire and eSATA. These will be easy to fit and your motherboard's manual will explain how.

Your case should have a manual that tells you how to take it apart and how to fit your components inside. Your case will generally ship with the screws that you'll need to fit your motherboard and other peripherals. If your case requires hard disks and optical drives to be fitted on runners, look for these in an accessory box either inside the packaging or the case itself.

If you're installing a graphics card, look inside its box carefully. Here you'll probably find DVI-to-VGA adaptors, which you'll need if you have a monitor with analogue inputs only; Molex-to-PCI Express power adaptors, which you'll need if your power supply doesn't have the necessary power connector; and, if your card supports it, DVI-to-HDMI adaptors. In the case of AMD graphics cards, this last item is really important. You have to use the AMD DVI-to-HDMI adaptor in order to get the sound working correctly; a standard adaptor will only deliver the picture.

Look inside all the component boxes for driver CDs. You can use these to get your hardware installed, although it's best to follow our guide on downloading the latest drivers on page 12 before you start building.

OPERATING THEATRE

A computer is useless without an operating system, so make sure that you've got your Windows or Linux disc handy before you begin building your computer.

A Windows install CD is made by Microsoft, bears a holographic Microsoft logo and has all the files needed to install the operating system. You can also use this CD to recover damaged Windows installations if you have trouble later on.

Your software box should also contain the licence key that you'll need to install Windows. You'll need this key when you install your operating system and if you ever have to reinstall Windows or contact Microsoft for support. It's critical, therefore, that you keep this key somewhere safe; without it, you'll need to buy a new copy of the software. Our complete guide to installing Windows 7 on page 86 explains everything.

To install Linux on your new computer, you'll first have to create an installation CD. This is easy to do, and our guide to installing Linux on page 100 explains everything you need to know.

SAVE IT FOR LATER

When you build your PC, you'll find that you may be left with some spare parts, such as blanking plates for expansion cards and extra drive rails for more hard disks. We recommend that you keep these parts somewhere safe, as you may need them should you decide to upgrade your computer in the future. It's also worth keeping any spare screws, as you never know when they'll come in handy.

TOOL UP

Building a PC isn't a particularly complicated procedure, and you'll need only a few tools to complete the job successfully. The picture opposite shows you the most common tools that you'll need, and you shouldn't need anything more specialised. Our guide to essential building skills on page 10 will show you how to use these tools, and our guide to your workspace on page 8 shows you the kind of area in which you should work.

ESSENTIAL TOOLS

No 2 crosshead screwdriver	£1.50
Long-nose pliers	£4.50
Multi-head screwdriver	£9
Total	**£15**

www.screwfix.com

OPTIONAL TOOLS

Torch	£6
Cable ties	£3
www.screwfix.com	
8GB flash drive	£9
www.aria.co.uk	
Thermal paste	£3
Anti-static wristband	£3
www.play.com	
Total	**£24**
TOTAL AMOUNT	**£39**

toolkit

RECOMMENDED
Hardware tools

MULTI-HEAD SCREWDRIVER
A ratchet or electric screwdriver with a wide range of fitments should cover anything that a standard crosshead screwdriver can't. Choose one with a range of hex sockets that includes at least 5, 6 and 7mm sizes.

CABLE TIES (not pictured)
Great for tidying the inside of your PC, or to clip groups of wires or loose components out of the way while you work. Longer ties are more expensive but more versatile, and you can snip off any extra length.

ANTI-STATIC BAG Use a large anti-static bag as a safe surface for working on any sensitive components. Smaller bags are ideal for storing or transporting components. Most PC parts arrive in anti-static packaging, so don't throw them away.

MEDIUM CROSSHEAD SCREWDRIVER
This can be used for almost every screw inside a PC, allowing you to fit or adjust all the major components. Choose one with a long shaft so that you can reach recessed screws.

TORCH This can be particularly useful when connecting a PC under a desk or making adjustments inside its case. A torch will also help you to read text on those components inside your PC that are labelled with small text or simply stamped with information.

FINE PLIERS You can use these to remove and fit jumpers, hold parts in tight spaces and help extract bits that are reluctant to move. You can also use them to cut wires or cable ties, and twist out metal blanking plates from a drive bay.

ANTI-STATIC WRISTBAND
Wearing this reduces the chances that static electricity will damage sensitive components such as your expansion cards, motherboard, memory or processor.

STORAGE DEVICE A simple USB flash memory device lets you transfer any drivers or patches you need from another PC. A larger hard disk device is perfect for taking full backups if you're transferring data and programs from another PC.

THERMAL PASTE
You may need this for the trouble-free installation of a new processor or graphics card heatsink, or when transferring a processor to a new motherboard. Make sure that you don't buy thermal adhesive by mistake.

Your workspace

1 DESK
You need a clear desk or table to work on your PC. As cases can have sharp edges, put down a cloth before you start work to prevent scratches. If you haven't got a suitable cloth, lining your desk with paper should do the job.

2 PLASTIC CUP
Screws and clips from inside your case can easily get lost. A plastic cup is a handy way of storing everything so you don't lose them.

3 RADIATOR
It's good to work near a radiator, so you can touch an unpainted part of it to discharge static. Alternatively, wear an anti-static wristband.

4 LAMP
A desk lamp will help make sure that you have enough light inside your PC.

5 MANUALS
Keep any manuals that came with your kit handy, as they'll help you build your PC correctly.

6 COMPONENTS
Keep your components in or on top of their anti-static bags until you're ready to use them.

Essential skills

BEFORE YOU UNWRAP all the shiny new components you've bought and start shoving them into your case, there are some safety lessons to learn, along with some key skills that will make building your PC much easier. Without these, you run the risk of damaging your computer before you've even turned it on. The worst part is that most of the time, you'll be unable to tell that you've caused any damage until you turn on your PC for the first time. At this point, tracking the problem down can be a real nightmare. We'll take you through the main pitfalls you'll face when building a new computer and, more importantly, how to avoid them.

STATIC

We all know about static electricity: it's the charge that builds up when we walk across a carpet and discharges when we touch someone else. This little flash of electricity may not seem very powerful, but it's potentially fatal for sensitive electronic components. Get a build-up of static and touch your processor, and you may have destroyed one of the most expensive parts of your computer before you've even started.

Fortunately, avoiding problems isn't that hard. If you've got one, wear an anti-static wrist strap. This will prevent static electricity from building up, making it safe to touch any component in your computer. If you haven't got one, don't panic, as there are other ways around the problem. Try to work near a radiator. To discharge any build-up of static, simply touch the unpainted part of the radiator. You're then safe to work.

Finally, all computer components come in anti-static bags to protect them. Don't remove any component from its bag until you're ready to fit it.

MAGNETIC SCREWDRIVER

Inside your PC, you'll find that there are lots of parts of your case that are awkward to reach to screw components into place. The easiest way to deal with this problem is to use a magnetic screwdriver. Simply place the screw into the screwdriver and then manoeuvre the screw towards its destination. The opposite is true when removing screws, as a gentle action should mean that a screw comes away attached to the screwdriver, rather than dropping to the floor.

Don't worry about magnetically sensitive devices inside your PC. A magnetic screwdriver isn't powerful enough to cause any damage or wipe any data.

THE RIGHT SCREWS

While the right screwdriver can make your job easier, it's essential to use the right screws to prevent damage. Put a screw that's too long into a hard disk, for example, and you could damage a circuit board and break the whole thing. Where possible, you should use the screws that come with the device, as these are guaranteed to work. Failing that, if your case has special fittings for devices, such as rails for hard disks and optical drives, the correct screws should have been fitted.

Of the different types of screws that are used, the small stubby ones are for hard disks and optical drives, the long screws are for holding expansion cards in place, while the screws with the flat heads are for fitting the motherboard and for some case panels. At all times, make sure that you don't overtighten screws, or you could cause damage. The idea is to tighten screws to the point where your components are held snugly in place.

⬆ Prevent the build-up of static by wearing an anti-static wrist strap

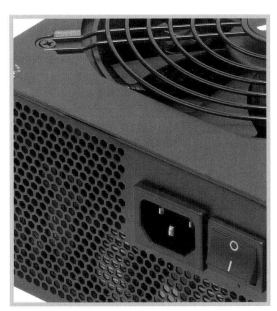

↑ Choose the right screw for the right job

↑ Check that the cables are all plugged in

THE RIGHT AMOUNT OF FORCE

When you plug components such as expansion cards, memory and a processor into your motherboard, it can be difficult to know how much force you should apply. Our tips should help you get it right. First, make sure that you've lined up your components correctly with the slot or socket – our step-by-step guide to building your PC in chapter 4 will show you how to do this.

Next, make sure that you're applying equal pressure across the device to move it into position. Processors should drop into place with little pressure, memory needs a firm push to click it into place, while expansion cards need a fair push. If you meet a lot of resistance, stop what you're doing and start again.

POWER CABLES

When building a PC, it's important to remember you're dealing with an electrical device. Before you plug the power in and turn on your computer, check that you've plugged in all the power cables properly, particularly on the motherboard. Loose connections can cause problems.

The fans inside a PC can cause problems, too, particularly if you've got power cables near them. Make sure that all power-carrying cables are clipped out of the way of fans so that you don't cut through them. Power connectors plug in only one way, so if you can't get one in make sure that it's

the right way round. Forcing a connector in the wrong way will damage your devices irreparably.

Before you plug in your power cable, make sure your power supply unit, or PSU, is set to the correct voltage. Although they're rarely seen today, some supplies have a switch that changes the input voltage from 110V (US) to 230V (UK). If you've accidentally set it to 110V, the power supply will be damaged and your motherboard may be affected, too.

TAKE YOUR TIME

The best tip we can give is to follow each step carefully and take your time. Building a PC isn't a race and, as you're dealing with lots of expensive components, it's best to get it right first time. Our easy-to-follow help will guide you through every step you need to take, while our troubleshooting guides in chapter 9 will help fix any problems you may encounter.

→ A magnetic screwdriver is a PC builder's best friend

Finding and installing drivers

ANY NEW HARDWARE you buy will come with a driver disc, so that you can install it easily. Some motherboards even have fancy installation wizards that automatically detect which drivers you need and install them automatically. However, while this sounds straightforward, the drivers that you get on the disc are usually out of date.

If you already have a working computer, your first job is to go online and download the latest driver files, saving them to a USB key or external hard disk. If you don't have access to a PC, don't worry. Simply use the drivers that came on the disc until your new computer is working, and then follow these instructions to download the latest drivers and install them afterwards. Thanks to the internet, getting drivers is incredibly easy and shouldn't take too long.

MOTHERBOARDS

The motherboard is the main part of your PC and it comes with plenty of built-in features, including onboard sound, networking, storage drivers and potentially even graphics. Windows will have drivers for many of these things, but if you want the best performance and the best range of features, you'll need the latest drivers.

You can get everything for your motherboard from the manufacturer's website: you'll find the address in your motherboard's manual. If not, then use a search engine to find the URL.

Once you're on the website, there should be a link for Support. Just keep following the links for motherboards and drivers. Eventually, you'll get to a point where you'll need to enter the details of your motherboard to locate the driver download page for your model. It's vital you get exactly the right model in order to get the correct drivers for your computer. If you can't find the details on the box or in the manual, then the motherboard's name is usually written on the board itself.

After you've entered your motherboard's details, you'll be presented with a long list of drivers divided by type, such as graphics or networking. For each heading, download one driver, making sure that you select the latest version. Most driver packages cater for all versions of Windows, but check the details to ensure that you download the correct driver.

GRAPHICS CARDS

If you're using onboard graphics, you'll be able to find the latest drivers on the motherboard

↑ AMD gives you a choice of files to download, but the full Catalyst Control Suite is the best choice for new computers

↑ You'll need to perform several file downloads to get the latest motherboard drivers

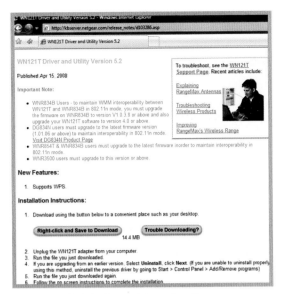

↑ You can find the latest drivers for all your devices on the internet

↑ Nvidia has a unified driver architecture, so a single download is all you need

manufacturer's website. If you're using a dedicated graphics card, you should download the drivers directly from AMD's or Nvidia's sites. This will ensure that you get the best performance and stability from your graphics card.

NVIDIA

Nvidia uses a unified driver package, so one download will work for most of its graphics cards. This makes installation simple. Visit *www.nvidia. com* and select Download Drivers from the Download Drivers menu in the top-left of the screen. Select the type of card (GeForce for consumer graphics cards) and the series of card that you have, such as 9xxx series for a GeForce 9600 GT. Select your language as English (UK) and click Search. Tick the box to accept the licence agreement and click Download.

It's important to select your graphics card model, as not every driver package has the driver for every graphics card. If you download the wrong package, your card won't install.

AMD (FORMERLY ATI)

AMD has a similar unified driver architecture to Nvidia. Visit *http://support.amd.com/us/Pages/ AMDSupportHub.aspx* and click the Download graphics drivers link under Support & Drivers. On the next page, select which operating system you'll be installing, select Radeon from the list (consumer graphics cards are all Radeon models), and then select your card. Click Go to be taken to the driver page. The Catalyst Software Suite includes the driver and the Catalyst Control Panel for configuring settings. Make sure you select your

model from the list, or you may get a version of the driver that doesn't support your card.

OTHER DEVICES

If you're installing other hardware, such as a wireless network adaptor, TV tuner, sound card or printer, you'll need to download the latest drivers for these, too. In a similar way to the procedure we've described above, you'll need to visit the manufacturer's website and follow the links until you get to where you can select the device for which you want to download drivers.

Check the device's manual for full details on the manufacturer's website. If you can't find any information, a Google search for the manufacturer's name should bring up the details you need. Remember to make sure you get the right driver for your device and your OS.

REGULAR CHECKS

Once you have the latest drivers, your job isn't done. You should regularly check manufacturers' websites and see if updates are available. Typically, graphics card drivers are updated monthly, while other devices are updated less regularly.

Driver updates fix known problems and can help your PC become more stable and perform better. It's worth going back to a manufacturer's site to check for updates if you're suffering a problem, as a new driver can often fix this.

Manufacturers' websites are also useful if you want help with a product. You can also find manuals for download, which can be really helpful if you lose your printed version and need to check a detail or plan an upgrade.

TIP

New versions of drivers can sometimes fix problems with your computer. If you're having trouble with a particular device, look for a newer driver before doing anything else.

CHAPTER 2

CHOOSING YOUR OPERATING SYSTEM

WHILE THE CHOICE of hardware may seem the most important decision when building a PC, it's the operating system that dictates how you'll use your computer. Depending on the type of PC you want, there's a choice between Windows and Linux. Here, we'll take you through the options so you get a system you're happy with.

IN THIS CHAPTER

Windows 7   16

Windows 7 editions   18

Linux   22

Windows 7

WINDOWS 7 IS Microsoft's latest operating system, and it's everything that Windows Vista should have been. Launched in 2009, it's the ideal choice for any new PC, and we wouldn't recommend choosing Windows Vista or XP unless you have an old copy of either of these two operating systems that you really want to use. With Windows 7 you're buying an operating system that's going to enjoy Microsoft's full support for the next few years.

When Windows Vista was first released, it had several compatibility problems. In particular, some hardware didn't have drivers for Vista, and some older software refused to run on the operating system. With Windows 7, this isn't the case: everything that worked on Vista – which is practically everything now – will work on Windows 7, so you can buy it safe in the knowledge that you won't have any compatibility problems.

Security became a major concern in Vista, but has been significantly improved in Windows 7. It also loads much faster and is less sluggish than Windows Vista. All round, it's a much better operating system. You're sure to be happy with your choice if you go with Windows 7.

FRIENDLY FIRE
Not all the new features are hidden under the surface. A lot of work has been put into making Windows easier to use and better to look at. This shouldn't be underestimated, as Windows 7's look and flash graphics mean it's a lot friendlier and make XP and even Vista look dated.

The new Windows management interface lets you quickly resize windows, see your desktop and choose which application you want to switch to.

Vista's sidebar has gone, but you can still run the same Gadgets (small applications for a specific job, such as showing the current weather, displaying post-it notes and showing you the current time). There are loads of Gadgets to choose from, with both official Microsoft and third-party applications available.

Those used to Vista will be pleased that there's still the built-in search, which makes it easier to find your files and programs. Simply click on the Start menu and start to type, and you'll be presented with a list of files and programs that contain your search terms. This search integrates with email (Windows Mail in Vista), so all your important information is incredibly easy to find. If you want Vista to search other email clients, such as Mozilla's Thunderbird or scan new file types, you can download iFilters (*http://ifilter.org*) to add these capabilities.

Windows 7 adds a lot more features besides, including Homegroups for easier networking, Blu-ray disc burning and full image-based backup in every edition. For more information, see our full guide to installing Windows 7 in chapter 6.

VERSION THERAPY
Windows Vista offered a relatively simple choice of just two versions, Home and Professional. However, Windows 7 comes in three major retail versions: Home Premium, Professional and Ultimate. The main benefit over Vista is that each edition contains the same features as the lower version, plus some additional options. You can also use Windows Anytime Upgrade (see page 114) to upgrade your existing edition without having to reinstall the operating system.

DETAILS

Microsoft Windows 7

WEB
www.microsoft.com

PRICE (these are for full editions that can be transferred to a new PC)
Home Premium £110
Professional £160
Ultimate £160

GOOD FOR
Mid-range or faster PC, Media Center computer

MINIMUM REQUIREMENTS
800MHz processor, 512MB memory, 40GB hard disk, DirectX 9-compatible graphics card for Aero interface

---

PROS Easier to use than XP; more stable than Vista; Media Center is built in
CONS Needs a lot of memory to run smoothly; doesn't support all old hardware and software

---

VERDICT
Easier to use, more secure and with better support than Windows Vista, Windows 7 is the operating system we've been waiting for. Unless you have a good reason to use another version of Windows, we recommend Windows 7.

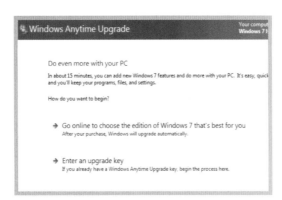

↑ You can upgrade your version of Windows 7 without having to reinstall all your programs and files

↑ Media Center is the easy way to view photos, videos and pictures, and record TV programmes

Windows 7 Home Premium is probably the best version for home users. Professional, as the name implies, has extra features for businesses, while Ultimate has all the features of both other editions plus the BitLocker drive encryption feature. Both versions are relatively expensive compared to Windows 7 Home Premium, though, and we don't think that they're worth the extra cash. You can use Microsoft's website to make sure the version you've chosen has all the features you need (*http://tinyurl.com/comparewin7*).

Finally, you also get a choice between the 32-bit and 64-bit versions of Windows. The 64-bit version of Windows can handle more system memory; the 32-bit version is limited to using a maximum of around 3.5GB. With most hardware and software supporting the 64-bit edition of Windows, there's little reason not to go for this unless you have a specific bit of hardware you know will work only with 32-bit Windows.

UNDER CONTROL

One of the key benefits of Windows 7 is that it comes with Windows Media Center. This application lets you watch and control you music, videos and photos using a remote control (which costs around £15) using a TV-friendly interface. If you add a TV tuner (also around £15), you can even turn your PC into a hard disk recorder, complete with an excellent – and completely free – electronic programming guide (EPG).

It's incredibly easy to configure Media Center, and the updated version supports Red Button services for interactive digital TV and Freesat HD broadcasts, neither of which were supported by Vista's version of Media Center.

⬆ Windows Homegroups makes connecting more than one PC over a network easy

⬆ Windows 7's new interface makes the operating system even easier to use

TIP

The Original Equipment Manufacturer (OEM) version of Windows 7 is designed for system builders. You don't get any telephone support, and can't transfer the licence to a new PC, but the software is considerably cheaper than the full boxed products, and cheaper than the upgrade version.

GOING STREAMLINE

Microsoft stuffed Vista full of extras such as the Windows Photo Gallery for organising photos. While some of these applications were useful, they added to the general bloat of the operating system. With Windows 7, Microsoft has gone for a more streamlined operating system and any extra applications are optional: you can either download similar applications to Vista's from Windows Live or install your own third-party programs instead.

POWER UP

Windows 7 will work with any computer on which Windows Vista would run. It needs a fairly decent specification and we strongly recommend that you have a PC with at least 2GB of memory in order to get the best experience. This means that Windows 7 isn't ideal if you want to build a budget PC; for this, consider using Linux (see page 22).

You may also find that older hardware such as printers and scanners won't have Windows 7 drivers, but this is unlikely to be a problem for most people. If you have a particular bit of kit you want to keep using and you can't find Windows 7 or Vista drivers, then XP could be a better choice if you've got a copy. For everyone else, Windows 7 is the operating system we've all been waiting for.

Windows 7 editions

SETTING ASIDE ENTERPRISE options, which are available only on corporate licences, there are four versions of Windows 7. Three are available both to upgraders and to purchasers of new PCs. The Starter edition, which is sold only with netbooks, is designed to provide the Windows 7 experience without overtaxing the slow processors typically used in low-end machines. This leaves netbook makers with little excuse to carry on bundling the older, cheaper Windows XP.

The three remaining editions are also available in 'N' versions. These are identical but for the omission of Microsoft's Windows Media Player, and have been made available to resolve an EU competition law dispute. Since they have fewer features but cost the same, they're not a good buy.

So you're left with a simple choice between Home Premium, Professional and Ultimate. If you're buying a new PC, it's most likely to come with Home Premium, but the supplier may be able to offer higher editions on request. For those buying just the software, there's a choice of full or upgrade packs. The upgrade is suitable for any PC running a licensed copy of Windows XP or Vista; you'll only need the full version for a machine that's never had Windows before, such as an Apple Mac (recent models can run Windows in addition to the Mac OS), or one whose copy of XP or Vista was obtained illegally and thus won't pass the upgrade check. If you bought a Windows Vista PC in 2009, you may have received a voucher for a completely free upgrade to Windows 7.

Choosing an upgrade pack doesn't prevent you opting for a 'clean' install of Windows 7, so you can start from scratch rather than updating your existing operating system. You get the same options; the only difference is that you have to boot your PC in Windows XP or Vista so the system can ensure your version is genuine.

FAMILY PACK

For the first time, Microsoft has issued a Family Pack for Windows 7. This is designed to make it easier and cheaper for a whole household to upgrade its PCs from previous versions of Windows, which makes a lot of sense when so many of the new features, such as HomeGroup, are aimed at homes with multiple computers all running Windows 7. The Family Pack costs around £130 and covers three machines. It's an upgrade rather than a full version – logically enough, since if you were buying a new computer you'd get Windows 7 pre-installed – and will be available only for Home Premium.

If you have three or even two PCs, the Family Pack can save you money, and you can upgrade to a higher edition later if you prefer through Anytime Upgrade. Microsoft has said the Family Pack will be available in 'limited quantities', but at the time of writing there's no sign of it running out.

STARTER EDITION

Windows 7 Starter Edition is available only pre-installed on new PCs, invariably low-cost netbooks. Some of the omissions, such as see-through windows and Taskbar previews, are justifiable on performance grounds. Others, including media streaming, Media Center and the

> **TIP**
> Once you've installed Windows 7, you can upgrade your edition whenever you like. Type 'anytime upgrade' into the search box, click Windows Anytime Upgrade and an Advisor guides you through the versions. You can then buy a new product key to unlock all the features of your chosen edition; some will already be on your PC but hidden, while the rest can be downloaded. Upgrading from Starter to Home Premium costs £70, from Home Premium to Professional £120, and from Professional to Ultimate £125. You can also buy boxed Anytime Upgrades from shops, which may be cheaper.

ability to change your desktop background, seem a bit mean. Nor is there support for multiple displays, so although you can plug your netbook into a monitor (assuming it has a suitable output), you can't use both screens at once.

Although Starter is a perfectly respectable operating system, most people will find it frustrating to use on a regular basis. If you have the choice, go for Home Premium instead. Alternatively, you can try Starter first and use Anytime Upgrade to move to another version later.

HOME PREMIUM

Home Premium is the version that consumers – as opposed to business users – are most likely to encounter. It contains a range of tools and options that will appeal to home users and anyone who uses their PC for entertainment purposes.

Prime among these is the revamped Windows Media Center. This can be used as a full-screen entertainment system and can even be operated entirely with a remote control from the comfort of your sofa. It also works with Media Center Extender devices, such as Logitech's Squeezebox Duet and Microsoft's own Xbox 360 console, so your PC can be your home's entertainment hub.

We've also been impressed by the much-improved Windows Media Player, now in version 12. This is a superb way to control a large music and video collection, thanks to its intuitive interface and media-streaming abilities.

The latest Windows Aero interface, which is only partially supported in Windows 7 Starter Edition, is fully installed in Premium, and it's not just there to look pretty but to make using your computer more intuitive. It's the little touches, such as easy ways to manage windows and some excellent desktop themes, that make it superior to Vista. If you're fortunate enough to have a touchscreen PC, things go a step further thanks to a full set of multitouch features.

More powerful options are missing from Home Premium, however: there's no BitLocker disk encryption, no Remote Desktop, and no Windows XP Mode to get the oldest and fussiest programs working (though most Windows XP software will run without problems). The Backup and Restore Center lacks the versatility provided by the Professional and Ultimate editions, and is

limited to local hard disk and DVD backups. These should be sufficient for most users, though.

Most personal users will be well served by Home Premium, but we recommend that power users, corporates and tweakers consider Ultimate.

PROFESSIONAL EDITION

Windows 7 Professional is aimed at businesses, but may also appeal to ambitious home users looking for more power than Home Premium offers. The enhanced Backup and Restore Center allows you to schedule automatic backups to a network-attached storage (NAS) device, while the Encrypting File System adds a layer of protection for sensitive files using complex algorithms that are almost impossible to crack.

The Professional edition also includes Windows XP Mode: an ingenious 'virtual machine' that lets you run Windows XP alongside Windows 7 so seamlessly you can forget which operating system a program is using. This will suit organisations that have invested in XP software that won't run correctly under Windows 7. It relies on Microsoft Virtual PC, which you can add as a free download.

ULTIMATE EDITION

Living up to its title, the Ultimate edition contains every feature from the Home Premium and Professional versions, plus some extras on top. In particular, the AppLocker and BitLocker security tools are unique to this version. The former restricts which applications can run on a network, and the latter offers full-disk encryption to ensure no-one can get their hands on your data. BitLocker to Go also enables encryption of USB sticks and other portable devices, ensuring your data stays confidential if a portable drive is misplaced.

If you're looking for supreme power and every feature on the block, then Windows 7 Ultimate is for you.

32-BIT v 64-BIT WINDOWS

Windows comes in 32- or 64-bit versions. The only significant difference between the two from a user's point of view is that the 32-bit version is limited to using 3GB of RAM. However, some older programs and peripherals may not work properly with the 64-bit edition. If you're upgrading an older PC, you'll also need to check that its processor is compatible with 64-bit Windows.

1&1 WEB HOSTING

ENHANCE YOUR WEBSITE W

When it comes to your website, functionality is everything. Enhance your hosting package with **easy-to-use 1&1 Click & Build Applications**. From blogging and newsfeeds to publishing pictures, getting more from your website has never been easier. Our comprehensive hosting packages include everything you need for online success:

✓ **65 Free 1&1 Click & Build Applications**
WordPress, Joomla, Gallery, phpBB, Moodle and many more!
Software and security updates included.

✓ **Design Software**
Adobe® Dreamweaver® or NetObjects Fusion® 1&1 Edition.

✓ **Double Security**
Your website is simultaneously hosted in two high-tech data centres in secure locations.

✓ **24/7 Telephone Support**
Plus free e-mail support.

1&1 DUAL HOSTING

*Please note that the design software is available for download from the 1&1 Control Panel. 12 month minimum contract term applies. Visit www.1and1.co.uk for full promotional offer details and terms and conditions. Prices exclude VAT.

Linux

LINUX HAS A reputation for being tricky to use and something that only those that like to mess around with command lines should even bother with. While to a certain degree this reputation is justified, Linux has come on leaps and bounds in the past few years, and is now arguably just as easy to install as Windows. It's also designed to make the most of a laptop or netbook's small screen, so you can also use it to improve an old portable computer as well as for a brilliant desktop operating system.

Linux, then, can be just as good a choice as Windows. Here we'll examine why you might want to install Linux on your new PC.

OPEN BORDERS

The main benefit of Linux is that it's free. As an open-source product, Linux costs nothing no matter what you use it for. The result has been that different companies have taken Linux and modified it to create their own versions, or distributions (distros), of the operating system.

The downside is that there are lots of different versions to choose from, each with its own slightly different installation routine and slightly different way of working. While this can be confusing, we recommend Ubuntu (*www.ubuntu.com*). This manages to strike a good balance between ease of use and power, and is a popular choice within the Linux community.

A FAMILIAR ENVIRONMENT

If you decide to install Linux, you'll find that you end up with a desktop that doesn't look a million miles away from Windows. In fact, from the

Launcher on the left of the screen you can select Home and browse through your files using a Windows Explorer-style file manager. All the familiar drag-and-drop functions are available, and you can even create files and folders in the same way as with Windows. Using Linux from this point of view, therefore, is just as easy as using Windows.

As well as sharing a similar way of managing files, you'll find that Linux also shares a lot of applications with Windows, such as the free LibreOffice office suite and the Chrome (called Chromium here) web browser. What you may find surprising, though, is that using Ubuntu to install these applications is actually easier than it is with Windows. Using the Ubuntu Software Center application you can browse additional software to install from an easy-to-use menu. Ubuntu then automatically downloads any applications you want to install. Try to do that with Windows.

That said, there's no getting away from the fact that your Windows applications won't install on Linux. While you'll be able to find free open-source equivalents for most of your Windows applications, not every type of application will be listed. You may be lucky enough to find an application to download from the web, but there's no standard installation routine for Linux, so installing a new application can sometimes be difficult.

STAYING UP TO DATE

Just as with Windows, Ubuntu is at risk from malicious hackers looking to exploit security vulnerabilities in the operating system. Fortunately, Ubuntu also has its own free updates. A message

DETAILS

Ubuntu 11.04

WEB
www.ubuntu.com

PRICE
Free

GOOD FOR
Budget PC, mid-range PC

MINIMUM REQUIREMENTS
1GHz processor, 512MB RAM, 5GB hard disk space

PROS Free; simple application installation **CONS** Hardware support not as good as in Windows; poor games support

VERDICT
As it's completely free, Ubuntu is an attractive choice where cost is a primary concern. Even where this isn't the case, if you want a PC for the internet and office work, Ubuntu's great.

↑ The Linux desktop is similar to Windows

↑ Installing new applications is incredibly easy

pops up when new updates are ready to be installed. Clicking on it lets you select the updates you want to install, which are then downloaded automatically from the internet and installed on your computer. Ubuntu is therefore just as easy to use and keep updated as Windows is.

HARDWARE COMPATIBILITY

While you'll find that Ubuntu will install flawlessly on most computers, there are times when you'll have hardware that won't work properly as there aren't any drivers for it. Wireless network adaptors are a good example of hardware with which you can have problems. A fair number of hardware manufacturers make Linux drivers available on their websites. What you don't get, though, is a simple installation file to run. Instead, installing drivers can be a real pain. Fortunately, if you search the internet for help, you'll find lots of friendly sites and forums that can talk you through installation.

In general, before choosing to install Linux, you may be best off running Ubuntu from a CD first to see if you like the look and feel of the operating system. If you do decide to use it on your new PC, check that drivers are available for the hardware and peripherals that you'll want to use.

CONFIGURE IT OUT

Finally, although Linux has improved in leaps and bounds, there will be the odd times when it proves to be a bit tricky to deal with. Installing drivers is one such area, but there are other things that are difficult. Trying to troubleshoot problems in Linux can become very difficult, and sometimes there's no choice but to revert to a command line to get

▲ Familiar applications such as Firefox are the same in Linux as in Windows

something done. This shouldn't put you off, however, and if you're interested in tinkering with your new computer and want to learn some new skills, Linux is a good way to go.

CHARMED LIFE

It's hard not to be taken in by Linux's charms, especially as it's free. With Firefox and OpenOffice being so easy to install from within Ubuntu, it's a great choice for a budget or mid-range PC whose primary job is going to be browsing the internet, sending email and using office documents.

If you want a wider choice of applications, have lots of peripherals and other hardware, then Windows works out better. If you're building a higher-end PC, particularly if gaming is a consideration, you should also use Windows.

TIP You can run Ubuntu from the installation disc without installing it. This Live CD version of the operating system means that you can give it a try before installing it – so you can find out if you like the operating system and can get along with it before commiting to installing it on your hard disk.

▲ Linux's file browser is similar to Windows Explorer

▲ Linux is free, so it's great for a budget PC

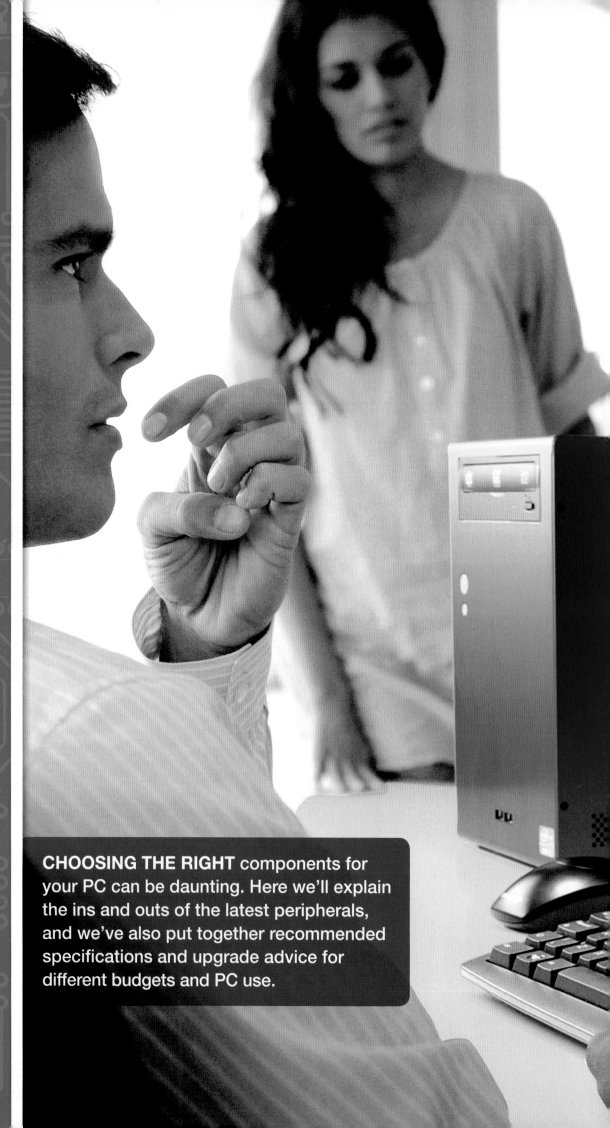

CHAPTER 3

CHOOSING YOUR HARDWARE

CHOOSING THE RIGHT components for your PC can be daunting. Here we'll explain the ins and outs of the latest peripherals, and we've also put together recommended specifications and upgrade advice for different budgets and PC use.

IN THIS CHAPTER

Choosing an AMD processor 26

Choosing an Intel processor 27

Choosing a motherboard 28

Choosing memory 30

Choosing a graphics card 31

Choosing a case 32

Choosing a power supply 32

Choosing a hard disk 33

Choosing an SSD 33

Budget PC 36

Mid-range PC 36

High-end PC 37

Extreme PC 37

Media centre PC 38

Mini PC 38

Essential peripherals 40

Choosing an
AMD processor

AMD'S PROCESSORS CAN'T match Intel's processors for speed at the high end, but for normal computers they strike a great balance between performance and price. For upgraders with existing systems, there's a great choice of processors availble in the AM3 format.

Before we look, we need to explain processors cores. A core is essentially a processor on a single chip. All modern processors have at least two cores (known as dual-core), so each processor really acts like two processors. This is brilliant for running multiple applications or for applications written to use multiple cores, such as video-editing suites. High-end processors have four cores (quad-core) or six cores and are even faster in video-editing applications and at running multiple programs. AMD also has some processors with three cores (tri-core).

SOCKET AM2+

Socket AM2+ processors have been phased out. Fortunately, if you have a Socket AM2 or AM2+ motherboard you want to use in your new PC, you can install a faster Socket AM3 CPU instead. You won't get quite the full speed, but it's better than having to replace the motherboard.

SOCKET AM3

Socket AM3 processors are being replaced by Socket FM1 chips. However, there's a wide range of CPUs available, making them a good choice for upgraders and budget-hunters alike. These processors can be used in older AM2+ motherboards and newer AM3 motherboards. If you buy an AM3 motherboard, you'll also need to buy DDR3 memory.

The AM3 processor range includes the Phenom II and Athlon II X2 (which are essentially Phenom processors with two cores) models. For a budget computer, we recommend an Athlon II X2 240 (around £44). If you want a bit more power, the Phenom II X2 550 Black Edition (around £80) is hard to beat, and this dual-core processor can also be easily overclocked.

For the best performance going, the Phenom II X4 955 Black Edition processor (around £90 including VAT) is a good choice, and it can also be overclocked easily. The six-core Phenom II X6 1090T (around £125) is even quicker. This is a great processor for intensive tasks such as video editing, but may be a bit excessive for a standard desktop computer.

SOCKET FM1

Socket FM1 is the latest processor type and is not compatible with other AMD processor sockets, so you'll also need a new motherboard. For this reason it's the best choice for new system builders.

The main benefit of the new processors is that they have fast onboard graphics built into the processor. This means you can do some light gaming without having to buy a dedicated graphics card; for Media Center PCs you end up with quieter computer.

There's not a lot of choice at the moment, but the quad-core AMD A8-3850 (around £103) is a great choice, it's fast in Windows and will handle games at lower detail settings. The quad-core A6-3650 (around £87) is a little slower, but will handle light gaming. Both processors can be used with a cheap AMD graphics card in hybrid CrossFire mode to boost gaming performance cheaply, giving a nice upgrade route.

↘ AMD's Llano processors combine performance with powerful graphics

Choosing an Intel processor

YOUR CHOICE OF Intel processors is defined by your motherboard's socket type (see page 28 for more information on choosing a motherboard). There are four main sockets: LGA775, LGA1366, LGA1156 and LGA1155. We'll explain each socket type in turn.

As we explained opposite, it's important to understand processor cores. A core is essentially a processor on a single chip. All modern processors have at least two cores (known as dual-core), so each processor really acts like two processors. This is brilliant for running multiple applications or for applications written to use multiple cores, such as video-editing suites. High-end processors have four cores (quad-core) and are even faster in video-editing applications and at running multiple programs.

LGA775 PROCESSORS

LGA775 processors have been phased out and aren't particularly good value even if you can find them, even for upgraders. If you already have an LGA775 motherboard, we recommend upgrading to LGA1155.

LGA1366 PROCESSORS

Older Core i7 processors use the LGA1366 socket. These are all quad-core or six-core processors, but a technology called HyperThreading makes the processor act like an eight-core or 12-core processor. These are the fastest processors you can buy, but you'll pay a high premium. We therefore don't recommend them for most people.

LGA1156 PROCESSORS

The LGA1156 standard is being replaced with LGA1155, but there are some good processors for upgraders. The CPUs come in Core i3, Core i5 and Core i7 variations.

The Core i5 and i7 processors support TurboBoost, which increases the processor's speed when it's under load, improving performance. The majority of processors use HyperThreading to virtually double the number of cores, while most processors also have graphics chips built in.

↗ The Core i3, i5 and i7 processors provide the ultimate in power

TIP Buy the right processor: new Intel LGA155 processors have four numbers in the model name; LGA1156 models have three numbers.

For a budget computer, the dual-core Core i3-540 (around £78) is the best choice, as it's very quick. The Core i5-760 is a true quad-core processor and gives incredible performance for around £160, but it doesn't have built-in grapics.

For the ultimate in performance, the Core i7-860 (around £230) is a great choice.

LGA1155 PROCESSORS

LGA1155 is Intel's latest processor socket and is the best choice for new builds. Again, there are Core i3, i5 and i7 models.

The dual-core Core i3 processors feature HyperThreading, but not Turbo Boost. Core i5 processors are quad-core with Turbo Boost, but not HyperThreading, while Core i7 processors are quad-core with HyperThreading and Turbo Boost. All models have built-in graphics that are good enough for Windows and playing films in Media Center. Processors with a K in the model name can be easily overclocked. For budget computers, the Core i3-2100 (around £85) is the best choice. For most people the Core i5-2500K (around £160) is ideal, while if you want the best performance, go for the Core i7-2600K (around £235).

ATOM PROCESSORS

Finally, Intel's Atom processors are low-powered models and perfect for entry-level computers or for network storage devices. The Gigabyte GA-D525TUD (around £48 including VAT) is the best choice as it's a motherboard and dual-core Atom 330 processor in one.

Choosing a Motherboard

THE MOTHERBOARD IS arguably the most important part of your computer, as it determines which processor, memory, graphics card and other components you can install.

SOCKET TO 'EM
The first choice is the socket type, as this defines which processors you can fit. If you're upgrading, you need the socket type to match your existing processor (unless you're upgrading the CPU as well); otherwise you need your motherboard to match your new processor choice. Intel LGA775 processors are out of date, so update your processor to a newer model at the same time as buying a new motherboard.

If you're looking for a new Intel LGA1156 socket there are a lot of good choices. Currently Intel's H55 chipset is the best, as it supports these processors' on-board graphics.

For older Core i7 processors, you'll need an LGA1366 socket. Intel's X58 chipset is currently the best choice.

For the latest Intel LGA155 motherboards, the Z68 chipset is the best choice, as it provides the best combination of features, performance and value. These chipsets support the processors' onboard graphics.

For AMD processors an AM2+ motherboard is hard to find now, so we recommend upgrading your processor and motherboard. AMD's AM3 motherboards can only take AM3 processors, but are a worthy upgrade. AMD's 790 chipset is a good choice for most people.

For the latest AMD FM1 processors, you'll need a motherboard with an AMD A75 chipset, as this is the only one currently available.

SIZE MATTERS
Motherboards come in two common sizes: ATX and microATX. ATX motherboards measure a maximum of 305x244mm and will fit in ATX cases only. MicroATX motherboards measure a maximum of 244x244mm and will fit in ATX and microATX cases. The main difference between the two types is that microATX motherboards have fewer expansion ports. Mini-ITX motherboards are designed for tiny cases, although the

↑ Make sure your chosen motherboard has enough spare ports

motherboards will also fit in most standard cases. Intel's destop Atom processors typically use Mini-ITX motherboards and are designed for lower-power computers.

EXPANDING OPTIONS
Make sure the motherboard you choose has enough SATA ports for hard disks, IDE ports for optical drives, and PCI and PCI-E slots for any additional expansion cards, such as a TV tuner, that you want to install.

Look for onboard graphics if you want to save money and aren't interested in playing games. If you want to play games and want the best-quality output for Blu-ray movies, then you should buy a dedicated graphics card. You'll need a PCI-E x16 slot to fit a dedicated card.

You can also buy motherboards with multiple graphics slots, which are certified for Nvidia's SLI or ATI's CrossFire technologies.

RECOMMENDED CHOICES
If you want an AM3 motherboard, we recommend the Gigabyte GA-970A-D3 (around £75). For AMD F1-based computers, we recommend the ATX Gigabyte GA-A55-DS3P (around £65). If you need a microATX motherboard, the Gigabyte GA-A55M-S2V (around £52) is a great choice.

For Intel systems, Gigabyte's GA-Z68XP-UD3P (around £130) is a great LGA155 ATX motherboard. If you want a microATX LGA155 motherboard, try the Gigabyte GA-Z68MA-D2H-B3 (around £100). If you have an LGA1156 processor, we recommend Gigabyte's ATX GA-H55-UD3H (around £91).

SIZE The size of your motherboard dictates the type of case it can go in. Most motherboards are either ATX or MicroATX. Match the board size to the type of case you want.

PROCESSOR SOCKET The processor socket must match the type of CPU you want.

MEMORY SLOTS These are for your PC's memory.

EXPANSION SLOTS Use these slots to attach TV cards, wireless adaptors and other peripherals.

USB HEADERS These let you connect your case's front-mounted USB ports.

SATA PORTS These are for hard disks and modern optical drives. Look for SATA3 ports for the fastest transfer rates.

Choosing Memory

MEMORY IS one of the most important components in your computer. The more you have, the better Windows will run, as it can keep all its data and applications in system memory; when Windows starts to run out of physical memory it begins using the hard disk as virtual memory, which is incredibly slow.

It's not quite as easy as buying the right type of memory and plugging it in, though, as you need to consider how much RAM you want and the configuration of it. Here, we'll explain your options.

MEMORY TYPE

The first thing you need to know is the type of memory that your computer needs, which will be dictated by the slots in your motherboard. Memory will be either DDR2 or DDR3: the types aren't interchangeable, so you need to make sure you buy the right one. You motherboard's manual and its manufacturer's website will let you know which memory you need to install.

A further clue is that Intel Core I3, i5 and i7, and AMD AM3 and FM1 motherboards all require DDR3 memory. Intel Core 2, Pentium Dual-Core and Celeron Dual-Core, and AMD AM2 motherboards all require older DDR2 memory. This is still in good supply and easy to find.

SPEED DEMONS

As well as buying the right type of memory, you also need the right speed. DDR2 memory comes in speeds of PC2-6400 (800MHz) and PC2-8500 (1,066MHz). For Intel systems, you need to buy the memory that is the closest match to the processor's front side bus (FSB) speed. You can fit PC2-8500 RAM in a system with an 800MHz FSB, but it will simply run a bit slower. For AMD systems that require DDR2 memory, you can fit PC2-8500 memory. You can expect to pay around £50 including VAT for 4GB of PC2-8500 RAM.

For DDR3 memory, there's PC3-6400 (800MHz), PC3-8500 (1,066MHz), PC3-10600 (1,333MHz) and PC3-12800 (1,600MHz). PC3-10600 memory is currently the best value and will work with all DDR3 processors. You can expect to pay around £40 including VAT for 4GB.

MEMORY BANK

Once you know which type of memory you need, you can choose how much RAM you want to install. We recommend a minimum of 4GB, but you should get more for better performance. Remember, there's a limit on the memory you can install. This is both set by the motherboard (check its specifications carefully) and by Windows.

If you have a 32-bit edition of Windows, it can only access around 3.5GB of memory (fit 4GB maximum); 64-bit versions of Windows have no practical limit, so you can fit more. That said, 8GB maximum should be enough for most people.

CONFIGURATION

All modern motherboards and processors support at least dual-channel memory. This works by sending memory data over two channels, and therefore increases performance. For this to work, you have to install memory in even numbers of modules, so for a dual-channel system with 4GB, you'd need two 2GB modules.

LGA1366 Core i7 processors use triple-channel memory, so you need to install memory in multiples of three. Most memory manufacturers will sell packs of memory with the required number of modules.

↓ Make sure you get the right memory for your chosen motherboard

Choosing a Graphics card

MANY MOTHERBOARDS AND modern CPUs have built-in graphics, but these deliver only basic games performance. For something a little more, you need a dedicated graphics card.

SIZE AND FEATURES

If you're building a media centre PC, a graphics card can be used to decode Blu-ray movies, leaving the processor free for other jobs. The chances are that you'll have a tiny case that accepts only a low-profile graphics card. There aren't many of these available; Asus's Radeon HD 6450 (around £32 including VAT) is the best choice.

The other factor you'll need to consider is how many slots a card takes up. The most powerful cards take up two expansion slots, so you can fit them only in large cases.

All modern graphics cards support HDCP, so you can plug them into an HD

TV and watch Blu-ray movies. If you don't have an HDMI output, you'll need a DVI-to-HDMI adaptor. For ATI cards you need to use the official ATI adaptor, or sound won't be transmitted over the connection. To make sure you get the necessary adaptor and cables, buy the full version of the card you want, not an OEM edition.

All modern graphics cards (ATI 6000 series and Nvidia 500 series) support PAP, so you can send Full HD Blu-ray sound to a compatible amplifier.

Finally, the most powerful modern graphics cards require an eight-pin PCI Express connector on your power supply.

RECOMMENDED CHOICES

For general high-performance gaming, the Asus Radeon HD 6950 (around £200 including VAT) is the best choice. The next step up is a big price jump for the most powerful graphics cards. The Asus Radeon HD 6990 card is the fastest you can get. At around £540 it's very expensive, but if you want no-holds barred performance for the ultimate in HD gaming, it's the best.

POWER Make sure your power supply has the necessary connectors. You can convert Molex to six-pin PCI-E, but you'll need dedicated eight-pin connectors if your card requires it.

SIZE Double-height cards require two free slots in your case, while low-profile cards can have the front bracket changed to fit in a small case.

DVI This is a common digital connection, and can be converted to VGA, DisplayPort or HDMI.

HDMI HDMI outputs take sound and video and are ideal for use in a media centre PC. They can be converted to DisplayPort or DVI.

DISPLAYPORT This is the newest digital connection and can be converted to HDMI or DVI.

Choosing a
Case

YOUR CASE DEFINES what your computer looks like, how many components you can fit inside and even the size of motherboard and type of graphics card that you can fit. Here's what to look out for.

SIZE OF THE PRIZE
The most important factor is the size of motherboard that you can fit. Most cases can take a full-sized ATX motherboard (see page 28 for more information). However, some cases can accept only microATX motherboards, while some specialist cases are designed for tiny Mini-ITX motherboards.

Larger cases can take smaller types of motherboard, but not the other way round, so make sure that you buy a case big enough for your motherboard.

COMPONENTS
Another important factor you'll need to consider when choosing a case is the number of components that you'll be able to fit inside. Look for a case that has enough 3½ in drive bays for hard disks and enough 5¼in drive bays for optical drives.

The size of the case can also play an important part in deciding which expansion cards you can fit: media centre cases often have only enough room for low-profile graphics cards, which aren't very common.

RECOMMENDED CHOICES
More expensive cases are generally quieter, better looking and also easier to build. Choose well and you'll get a much better PC.

↑ Good-quality cases are quieter and better-looking than cheap models

The In Win Z638 microATX case (around £27 inc VAT) is a good choice for a budget computer. For something a bit sturdier, In Win's PE668T2 (around £41 including VAT) is a great choice. For a high-end computer, the In Win Dragon Rider (around £95 including VAT) is an excellent choice. For a media centre PC, try SilverStone's Grandia GD01 (around £100 including VAT).

Choosing a
Power supply

YOUR POWER SUPPLY brings your PC to life and ensures that there's enough power going to each component. Cheap power supplies are available, but in our experience they're unreliable, can break easily and often deliver unstable voltages that can crash a computer. Pick branded, more expensive models and it will save you money in the long run.

POWER UP
Your main choice when picking a power supply is getting one with the right power output, which is measured in Watts. For a basic entry-level PC, look for a 600W supply; for a mid-range or high-end PC, you'll need a 800W supply. For very powerful computers with lots of hard disks and powerful graphics cards, you should buy an 1,00W supply or higher.

The other thing to consider is the number of power connectors they have. Make sure your supply has enough SATA and Molex connectors for your computer.

Check that the supply supports your chosen graphics card; powerful modern graphics cards have eight-pin PCI Express connectors, and your power supply must have the matching connector for this to work. If you want to use ATI's CrossFire or Nvidia's SLI, look for a supply with multiple six- and eight-pin PCI Express connectors.

RECOMMENDED CHOICES
OCZ's ModXstream Pro 600W (around £55 including VAT) is a good entry-level

↑ Make sure your power supply has the right connectors for your PC

power supply. For a more powerful computer, try OCZ's ZX Series 850W (around £125 including VAT). Finally, for powerful, high-performance computers with a lot inside, OCZ's ZX Series 1,000W (around £155 including VAT) is an excellent choice.

Choosing a
Hard disk

YOUR HARD DISK stores your operating system, applications and all your data. Getting the right model is therefore incredibly important. The choice should be fairly simple, but here we'll explain what features to look out for.

FULL CAPACITY
All modern hard disks and computers use SATA interfaces. This makes your choice infinitely easier. Your primary consideration when buying a hard disk is to get a drive with the highest capacity you can afford. However, small and extremely large hard disks usually cost more per gigabyte, so aren't especially good value. Unless you're on a particularly tight budget, it's worth spending a few pounds more to get a larger, better-value disk.

Finally, if you're planning to use RAID – where you use multiple hard disks to create one virtual disk with better performance, data protection or both – you should buy identical drives.

RECOMMENDED CHOICES
Hard disks have fallen a lot in price recently, so large disks are comparatively cheap. The smallest hard disk we would recommend is Samsung's 1TB SpinPoint F3, which costs around £45 including VAT; a 500GB hard disk will cost only a few pounds less and isn't worth it. For more capacity, Samsung's 2TB

↑ When choosing a hard disk, look for the highest capacity you can afford

SpinPoint EcoGreen F3 (around £60 including VAT) or Hitachi's 3TB Deskstar 7k3000 (around £135 including VAT) are both good value.

You can add as many hard disks as you'll need, but for the best performance consider an SSD (see below) to boot from and a regular disk for storage.

Choosing an
SSD

A SOLID STATE drive (SSD) is a hard disk replacement that has no moving parts, using flash memory over a spinning disc, making it more reliable. SSDs are also a lot faster than regular hard disks, making your computer more responsive and quicker to start. The downside of SSDs is that they come in relatively small capacities and are comparatively expensive per gigabyte. It's therefore worth buying an SSD to use as a boot disk and for applications, and using a standard hard disk for secondary storage.

CAPACITY CROWD
The main thing to look for is storage capacity. For installing Windows 7 and some applications, we recommend a minimum of 60GB, but look for 120GB or 240GB if you want to make sure you won't run out of disk space when installing new applications.

Not all SSDs are equal, and there are many cheap and slow products out there. Look for a drive with a SATA3 interface for the best performance, as well as one with a decent controller, such as the latest Sandforce model. These will give you the best performance.

MAKING THE UPGRADE
If you're looking to upgrade, SSDs are a brilliant way to add a little more performance to an existing computer. While you can try and clone your existing hard disk to your SSD, copying your existing operating system and applications, we don't recommend this. SSDs require a certain amount of special configuration, and Windows 7 supports many of the necessary commands. We therefore recommend that you have Windows 7 and perform a clean install, following our SSD configuration instructions (see page 64).

RECOMMENDED CHOICES
For the best performance, we recommend an OCZ Vertex 3 drive (around £190 for 120GB and £380 for 240GB). If you're on a tighter budget, OCZ Agility 3 drives are a good choice.

Your hard drive is holding you back.

OCZ Solid State Drives can transform your computing experience...

SSDs are faster

SSDs have 100 times greater throughput and instantaneous access times for quicker boot ups, and faster file transfer rates than hard drives. Get more done in less time for a state-of-the-art computing experience.

SSDs are Lighter

With no moving parts, SSDs are able to run quieter in ultra-lightweight mobile systems at only 77g vs. 52.5g for HDDs. SSDs won't weigh down your netbook or tablet PC when you're on the go!

SSDs are more responsive

Systems with SSDs feel snappier thanks to their incredibility fast access latencies. While HDDs are faster when the data you want is in the vicinity of the read/write heads, all parts of a SSD are accessed the same way... fast.

SSDs are Cooler

The energy-efficient storage upgrade to your desktop or laptop, SSDs require very little power to operate that translates into significantly less heat output by your computer.

SSDs are Cost-Efficient

Though still higher price/gigabyte than HDD, SSDs offer cost savings in the long run with lower energy usage and greater productivity with higher Input/Outputs (IOPS) with one SSD compared to a bank of hard drives for businesses.

SSDs are Quieter

With no moving parts, SSDs run at near silent operation and never disturb your computing experience during gaming or movies, unlike loud, whirring hard disc drives.

Award Winning Performance
Max Read: up to 550MB/s
Max Write: up to 520MB/s
4K Random Write: 60,000 IOPS
Available from 60GB to 480GB capacities

Maximum IOPS
Max Read: up to 550MB/s
Max Write: up to 500MB/s
Maximum 4K Random Write: 85,000 IOPS
Available from 60GB to 480GB capacities

Caching Solution
Max Read: up to 550MB/s
Max Write: up to 510MB/s
4K Random Write: 80,000 IOPS
Available in 64GB and 128GB capacities

OCZTECHNOLOGY.COM

Passion for Performance.

Available at: overclockers.co.uk ebuyer.com dabs.com   scan.co.uk

BUDGET PC

This budget computer will be good enough for basic computing tasks, such as photo editing and surfing the web. You can add a faster processor, install Windows 7 and add a better graphics card if you want a better PC.

SHOPPING LIST
Recommended minimum specifications

PROCESSOR	
AMD A6-3650	£87
(Intel Core i3-2100	£92)
MOTHERBOARD	
AMD: Gigabyte GA-A55M-S2V	£83
(Intel: Gigabyte GA-Z68MA-D2H-B3	£95)
CASE	
In Win Z638	£27
HARD DISK	
Samsung SpinPoint F3 1TB	£45
MEMORY	
4GB Corsair Value Select DDR3 PC3-10600	£21
OPTICAL DRIVE	
Samsung Super-WriteMaster SH-S223C	£15
OPERATING SYSTEM	
Ubuntu Linux 11.04	Free
POWER SUPPLY	
OCZ ModXStream Pro 600W	£55
TOTAL	**£303**

MID-RANGE PC

SHOPPING LIST
Recommended minimum specifications

PROCESSOR	
Intel Core i5-2500K	£166
(AMD A6-3650	£87)
MOTHERBOARD	
Intel: Gigabyte GA-Z68MA-D2H-B3	£95
(AMD: Gigabyte GA-A55M-S2V	£53)
CASE	
In Win Z638	£27
HARD DISK	
Samsung SpinPoint F3 1TB	£45
MEMORY	
8GB Corsair CMZ8GX3M2A1600C9	£46
OPTICAL DRIVE	
Samsung Super-WriteMaster SH-S223C	£15
OPERATING SYSTEM	
Windows 7 Home Premium	£110
GRAPHICS CARD	
Asus Radeon HD 6870	£160
POWER SUPPLY	
OCZ ZX Series 850W	£136
TOTAL	**£800**

This powerful computer will be able to cope with any application and its dedicated graphics card means that it can also play games. Look for a bigger hard disk and faster graphics card if you want more from your PC.

HIGH-END PC

This is a stunning PC that will be more than good enough for any job. There's little need to upgrade here, but a larger hard disk and faster graphics card could boost performance.

SHOPPING LIST
Recommended minimum specifications

PROCESSOR
Intel Core i5-2500k   £166
(AMD A8-3850   £103)

MOTHERBOARD
Intel: Gigabyte GA-Z68XP-UD3P   £130
(AMD: Gigabyte GA-MA785GMT-UD2H   £65)

CASE
In Win PE668T2   £41

HARD DISK
2TB Samsung SpinPoint F4   £58
(SSD: 120GB OCZ Vertex 3   £180)

MEMORY
8GB Corsair CMZ8GX3M2A1600C9   £46

OPTICAL DRIVE
Lite-On IHBS112-32   £70

OPERATING SYSTEM
Windows 7 Home Premium   £110

GRAPHICS CARD
Asus Radeon HD 6950   £200

POWER SUPPLY
OCZ ZX Series 1000W   £153

- -

TOTAL   **£974**

SHOPPING LIST
Recommended minimum specifications

PROCESSOR
Intel Core i7-2600k   £235
(AMD A8-3850   £103)

MOTHERBOARD
Intel: Gigabyte GA-Z68XP-UD3P   £110
(AMD: Gigabyte GA-MA785GMT-UD2H   £65)

CASE
In Win Dragon Rider   £95

HARD DISK
2TB Samsung SpinPoint F4   £58
SSD: 240GB OCZ Vertex 3   £380

MEMORY
8GB Corsair CMZ8GX3M2A1600C9   £46

OPTICAL DRIVE
Lite-On IHBS112-32   £70

OPERATING SYSTEM
Windows 7 Home Premium   £110

GRAPHICS CARD
Asus Radeon HD 6950   £200

POWER SUPPLY
OCZ ZX Series 1000W   £153

- -

TOTAL   **£1,457**

EXTREME PC

This PC is incredibly fast, but you're paying a lot of money for it. The graphics card will deliver the best games performance. If you want an even faster computer, look to buy better cooling and overclock the CPU.

MEDIA CENTRE *PC*

This system will give you plenty of disk space for digital TV recording, and the optical drive is capable of playing Blu-ray films. Arcsoft's TotalMedia Theatre 5 Blu-ray playback software costs around £70.

SHOPPING LIST
Recommended minimum specifications

PROCESSOR
Intel Core i3-2100 £92
(AMD A6-3650 £87)

MOTHERBOARD
Intel: Gigabyte GA-Z68M-D3 £83
(AMD: Gigabyte GA-A55M-S2V £53)

CASE
SilverStone Gradia GD01 £100

HARD DISK
Samsung SpinPoint F3 1TB £45

MEMORY
4GB Corsair Value Select DDR3 PC3-10600 £21

OPTICAL DRIVE
LG GGC H20L £76

OPTICAL DRIVE
Lite-On IHBS112-32 £70

OPERATING SYSTEM
Windows 7 Home Premium £110

POWER SUPPLY
OCZ ModXStream Pro 600W £55

- -

TOTAL £652

MINI *PC*

SHOPPING LIST
Recommended minimum specifications

PROCESSOR
Intel Atom D525 (integrated in motherboard)

MOTHERBOARD
Gigabyte GA-D525TUD £48

CASE
In Win BP655 £48

HARD DISK
Samsung SpinPoint F3 1TB £45

MEMORY
4GB Corsair Value Select DDR3 PC3-10600 £21

OPTICAL DRIVE
Lite-On IHBS112-32 £70

OPERATING SYSTEM
Windows 7 Home Premium £110

POWER SUPPLY
200W included with case £0

- -

TOTAL £342

This small PC won't take up much room on your desk, but it will be powerful enough for most tasks. It comes with a power supply and is great for internet and office use.

JUMP AND FEEL THE RUSH

ZT SERIES POWER SUPPLY

A superb choice for performance and power users who need solid, reliable PSU

- Newest OCZ power management solution
- Fully Modular
- 80 Plus® Bronze
- Powerful Single Rail
- Available in 550W, 650W, 750W

80 PLUS BRONZE

ZX SERIES POWER SUPPLY

Industrial-grade yet designed with enthusiasts, gamers and modders in mind.

- Triple VGA-Ready
- Fully Modular
- 80 Plus® Gold
- Powerful Single Rail
- Available in 850W, 1000W, 1250W

80 PLUS GOLD

ZS SERIES POWER SUPPLY

An affordable solution for driving today's value-oriented gaming systems.

- NVIDIA® SLI™ and ATI CrossFireX™ mode capability
- Compact Form Factor Design
- 80 Plus® Bronze
- Powerful Single Rail
- Available in 550W, 650W, 750W

80 PLUS BRONZE

The new power trio from OCZ lets you jump in head-first and push your system to the limit. Whether you're looking for an excellent value or the maximum wattage, OCZ PSUs deliver ultimate stability, high efficiency, and powerful Single Rail designs backed by a leading warranties for ultimate protection.

OCZ Technology
OCZTECHNOLOGY.COM

Passion for Performance.

Available at:

OCUK OVERCLOCKERS UK — overclockers.co.uk | ebuyer.com — ebuyer.com | dabs.com — dabs.com | SCAN — scan.co.uk

Essential peripherals

ALTHOUGH GETTING THE base specifications for your PC and choosing the right operating system is incredibly important, you should also start thinking about the other peripherals you want to use. If you're sitting in front of your computer all day, buying a decent monitor and a comfortable keyboard and mouse is incredibly important. Don't scrimp and save on the extra peripherals, as you'll end up not enjoying using your new PC. Here, we'll talk you through the options that are available to you.

MONITORS

The monitor is your window into your computer. When you use your PC, it's this display that you'll be staring at all the time. Getting one that produces a decent image and fits your needs is, therefore, incredibly important.

If you haven't bought a monitor for a while, you'll be surprised at the increased choice available. For starters, regular 'square' monitors are pretty much a thing of the past, and have been replaced by widescreen monitors. These make watching films more pleasant and make working with things such as large spreadsheets much easier. With wider resolutions than standard monitors, things such as Windows' Sidebar fit more comfortably on the screen and still leave plenty of rooms for documents.

Widescreen monitors, like standard displays before them, come in a range of different sizes and resolutions. At the bottom of the pile are budget 17in and 19in models, which have a 1,440x900 resolution. These typically start at less than £100. However, in our eyes they're not worth it. Instead, 24in monitors, such as liyama's ProLite E2409HDS-1, are larger and easier on the eye than 19in models and cost only a little more at around £140. The main benefit, however, is that most models have a resolution of 1,920x1,280, so you get a lot more information onscreen, and can watch Full HD video. In fact, with monitor prices so low, there's no point in buying a monitor that doesn't have a Full HD 1,920x1,080 resolution.

If you want to take the next step up, 27in monitors, such as AOC's e2795Vh, have a resolution of 1,920x1,080, and are even easier on the eye because of the larger display. For standard Windows use, this large desktop is a real pleasure to use.

↗ A 24in widescreen monitor is a great choice for a new PC, and can be picked up relatively cheaply

If money's no object, you can opt for an even larger resolution. Hazro's HZ27WC has an incredible 2,560x1,440 resolution, although at £420 it's also incredibly expensive.

When choosing a monitor, it's worth taking some time to decipher the specifications to make sure you get one suitable for your needs. The viewing angles (horizontal and vertical) denote the angle at which the picture starts to deteriorate when you're looking at the screen. Higher viewing angles are better, particularly if you want to use your monitor to show films to more than one person.

The brightness of a monitor is measured in candela per square metre (cd/m^2). The higher the number, the brighter the picture, so the easier your monitor will be to see. Brightness levels from $300cd/m^2$ should be chosen.

The contrast ratio of a monitor tells you the difference between the darkest shade (black) and the lightest shade (white) that the monitor can produce. Many modern monitors use dynamic contrast ratios, where the backlight is dimmed to increase the range of shades that can be produced. Typically, a monitor with a contrast ratio of 1,000:1 or higher should be able to produce dark blacks and bright whites.

The final specification that you'll come across is the response time. This measures how long it

TIP
If your PC has two graphics outputs – most graphics cards do – you can run two monitors together and split the Windows desktop over both.

takes the monitor to change a pixel from black to white and back to black, although some manufacturers 'cheat' and quote a grey-to-grey time. High response times imply that the picture will take a long time to change, so fast-moving action – as in games, for example – could end up with ghosting and smearing. In our extensive tests we've noticed that as long as a monitor has a response time of 25ms or lower, you won't see any problems. Don't get drawn into paying more money for a monitor just because it has an incredibly quick advertised response time.

The only other option to consider is the type of inputs you want on your screen. If the PC you're building has a digital DVI output, look for a monitor with a matching input. This will give you the best-quality picture. If you want to watch HD movies, then look for a monitor with an HDMI connection or HDCP support on its DVI input.

↗ The Desktop Wave's curved keyboard fits perfectly under your hands and makes typing easier

If your PC only has an analogue D-sub output, you'll need a monitor with one of these. Most monitors that support DVI also have a D-sub input, too. If you want to connect a games console or regular DVD player, you'll need a monitor with SCART, S-video, composite or S-video inputs. These are a lot rarer, though.

KEYBOARDS AND MICE

The keyboard and mouse remain the main way in which we interact with our computers. Buying the right set is crucial if you want to make your computer easy to use. The most cost-effective way to buy a new keyboard and mouse is to get a set that includes both.

Most sets include wireless peripherals. These are reliable and generally have long battery lives. There are no cables to clutter up your desk, and we highly recommend these products. The main choice you'll have to make is whether you want a regular keyboard or an ergonomic model.

Regular keyboards, such as Logitech's Cordless Desktop LX710 Laser (around £27 including VAT), are easiest for most people to use, as they place the keys in a straight line. For touch-typists, ergonomic keyboards can be better, as the keys are placed more naturally for the typing position. However, we've never got on very well with the full-on ergonomic models with the 'split' in the middle of the board. We've found that Logitech's Cordless Desktop Wave (around £42 including VAT) provides a decent balance between comfort and ergonomic design. It has a slight 'smile' to it, and each key is at a slightly different height to match the differences in finger

↑ A 27in monitor has a high resolution, which is perfect for Windows applications and films

CHOOSING YOUR HARDWARE

length. It's a great keyboard if you're going to be doing a lot of typing.

Although wireless mice are fine for using Windows, if you play a lot of games a wired mouse is a much better option. This is because wired models don't have as much lag, so each mouse movement is replicated instantly on the screen – essential if you want to get that accurate head shot. If you're a keen gamer, we'd recommend buying a dedicated gaming mouse, such as Razer's Death Adder (£40 including VAT).

Those who love playing the latest games should also consider buying a mouse mat, rather than using the surface of a desk. With the right mat, such as the ICEmat 2nd Edition (around £30), you'll get a low-friction surface, so your mouse will glide around effortlessly.

SPEAKERS

To get the best out of your computer, you need to invest in a decent set of speakers. Don't rely on those built into your monitor, as they'll never be able to produce the clean balanced sounds of a dedicated set. Fortunately, buying speakers doesn't have to be expensive.

First, work out what kinds of speakers you want. Standard 2.1 sets have two stereo speakers and a sub-woofer, which produces rich, thumping

→ These surround-sound speakers can connect to your DVD player as well as your PC, making them ideal for use in a home-entertainment setup

bass. If you primarily use your computer for music or games, then these kinds of speakers will suit your needs. The best set we've reviewed, Logitech's Z-523, costs around £50, and produces incredibly rich and detailed sound.

Next, you have the choice of surround-sound speakers. These are ideal if you want immersive sound around you when you're watching films and want to enjoy the full soundtrack, for example. Surround-sound speakers typically come in 5.1 or 7.1 speaker configurations, where the .1 is the bass sub-woofer and the 5 and 7 refer to the number of satellite speakers. To be honest, 7.1 sets aren't worth it unless you'll be using your computer in a massive room. Besides, the extra two speakers and cables mean that you're just adding clutter to your home. A 5.1 set will suit most people.

Again, there's a choice of sets to consider. Standard 5.1 PC speakers, such as Logitech's Z-506 (around £75), use analogue mini-jack plugs that connect to the sound card's outputs at the rear of your PC. To enjoy surround sound on your DVDs and HD movies, you'll need software capable of decoding the sound to analogue outputs. Windows Media Center will decode Dolby Digital soundtracks, but not DTS; CyberLink's PowerDVD will do all formats, but you'll need to upgrade to the full version from any 'lite' version that came bundled with your optical drive.

↑ A decent set of 2.1 speakers will produce rich sounds in games and music

Alternatively, buying a set of 5.1 speakers with a built-in decoder, such as Logitech's Z-906 (around £280), will enable you to connect your computer digitally to the speakers and let them do the hard work of decoding. For this to work, you'll need to have an S/PDIF output from your PC. The Z-906 speakers have optical and coaxial S/PDIF inputs and can decode Dolby Digital and DTS soundtracks. They also have 5.1 channel analogue inputs, so you could still let your PC do the audio decoding. The benefit of this system is that you can also connect your regular DVD player to the speakers, so you can use them for your home cinema setup, too.

TV TUNERS

With Media Center now built into Vista Home Premium and Windows 7, turning your PC into a fully fledged hard disk recorder simply requires you to add a TV tuner. With Media Center's excellent free programme guide, you'll find a PC the easiest hard disk recorder to use. When you make your choice, there are a few things to consider.

First, it's not worth buying an analogue-only tuner. The analogue TV service is being turned off over the next few years, leaving only digital TV. That said, if you can't get a very good reception for digital TV, look to get a hybrid tuner with both digital and analogue capabilities; this way you can use the best signal but still switch over to digital when the time comes.

The best choice for most people is a digital tuner. As Media Center can handle two tuners at once, allowing you to record one channel while watching another, it makes sense to buy a TV card with dual tuners. This doesn't have to be expensive, as the Hauppauge WinTV Nova-TD Diversity (£60) shows. This USB tuner plugs into a spare USB port, but you can also get internal tuners that plug into a spare PCI or PCI Express slot for similar money. The Diversity tag means the card can use both tuners to improve the quality of your TV reception. However, using it in Diversity mode means you can only watch a single channel, as with a single-receiver TV tuner.

Finally, Freesat now provides HD TV for free, and some cards give you this ability on your PC. In order to use the service, you'll need a satellite dish, such as those provided by Sky. An easier

option is to add a second tuner for Freeview HD (Media Center supports lots of tuners, so you can run two Freeview and one Freeview HD easily). The PCTV Systems DVB-T2 290e USB tuner (£90) is a good choice. This receiver has a single USB tuner for receiving one HD channel at a time.

↑ A dual tuner allows you to watch one TV channel while recording another

THE MAIN TASK you have when building a PC is making sure that you put all the components together correctly so that your new computer works first time. Our detailed step-by-step advice will help you put any PC together from start to finish.

CHAPTER 4
BUILDING YOUR PC

IN THIS CHAPTER

Taking the case apart   46

Installing the power supply   48

Installing the motherboard   50

Installing an Intel processor   56

Installing an AMD processor   57

Installing memory   58

Fitting the internal cables   60

Installing a hard disk   62

Installing an SSD   64

Installing an optical drive   66

Installing a graphics card   68

Installing expansion cards   72

Putting the case back
together   75

Taking the case apart

REMOVE THE FRONT Many cases require you to remove the front panel. Some simply lift off, but check for screws and clips inside.

SCREWS Most cases are held together by screws that need to be removed. Thumbscrews and clips, such as these, can be undone without a screwdriver.

HOW TO...
Take the case apart

1 REMOVE THE SIDES

Start by taking off the side panels to get inside the case. As noted on the diagram opposite, you may need to take the front panel off first to get at the screws to remove the side panels. Some cases, like the one pictured, have thumbscrews, so you don't even need a screwdriver. If your case has a second panel, make sure that you remove this, too, so that you can work on both sides of the case when you're inside it.

2 TAKE OUT INNARDS

Once you're inside your case, you need to check it for accessories. It's common for manufacturers to put spare screws, proprietary drive rails and instruction manuals inside. Take out everything that isn't screwed into place. Look for silica gel taped to the side as well. Remove any packaging so that you're left with a bare interior.

3 REMOVE OPTICAL DRIVE BLANKING PLATES

In order to fit your optical drive later, you may need to remove some plastic and metal blanking plates. If you haven't done so already, it's probably helpful to take off the front of the case. Your case's manual will tell you how to do this, but most cases simply unclip from the inside.

Look for the 5¼in drive bay into which you'll fit your optical drive. Match this up to the front panel. On some cases this will be the top one, which will have a flap to hide the optical drive from view, so you don't have to get a drive the same colour as your case. On other cases, you'll have a plastic blanking plate on the front panel that should unclip.

Inside the case, you'll find a metal blanking plate that you'll need to remove. By gently rocking it backwards and forwards, you should be able to break the connection. Be careful not to cut yourself doing this.

4 REMOVE FLOPPY DRIVE BLANKING PLATES

If you're planning to fit a memory card reader or floppy disk drive, you'll need to follow the same steps you did for the optical drive. Find the 3½in drive bay you want to use and break off the metal blanking plate. Next, pop out the corresponding plastic blanking plate on the front panel.

TIP
The inside of the case can have sharp edges, so be careful when you remove any blanking plates.

Installing the power supply

The ATX connector provides power to your motherboard

The SATA connector is for hard disks and optical drives

A standard PCI Express graphics card connector

The newer 8-pin PCI-E power connector

TIP
Tuck any unwanted cables out of the way inside the case to improve airflow and keep your PC tidy.

The secondary motherboard power connector

A connector for floppy disks and memory card readers

The Molex connector is for hard disks

HOW TO...
Install the power supply

1 FIT SUPPLY ON TO SHELF
If your power supply fits at the top of your case (some cases have space at the bottom), you'll see a small shelf for it to rest on. Slide the power supply on to this shelf and push it backwards until it makes contact with the back of the case.

2 SCREW IN SUPPLY
If your power supply is the correct way round, its screw holes will match up with those in the back of the case. If they don't, remove the supply and rotate it 180°. Use four screws to attach the power supply securely to the case.

Installing the motherboard

SATA PORTS These are for hard disks, newer DVD writers and Blu-ray drives.

EXPANSION SLOTS These are used for internal peripherals such as TV tuners and graphics cards.

IDE PORT (NOT PICTURED) For older DVD drives, but not all motherboards have

MEMORY SLOTS These are for your PC's memory.

PROCESSOR SOCKET For your processor.

REAR PANEL CONNECTORS These ports are fixed on your motherboard.

HOW TO...
Install the motherboard

1 UNPACK THE BOARD
Open your motherboard's box. You'll see lots of cables, a driver CD, a metal blanking plate with holes cut out and a manual. Take these components out and put them to one side, as you'll need them later on.

The motherboard will be inside an anti-static bag and resting on top of anti-static foam. Slide the motherboard out of the bag, but leave it attached to the foam for now. Place the motherboard and foam on top of the anti-static bag, and take out the metal blanking plate.

2 MEASURE BLANKING PLATE
The blanking plate fits into the case, and gives you access only to the ports that your motherboard has. However, some motherboard manufacturers use generic blanking plates that fit their entire range of boards. With these, you may need to remove some metal covers to give access to your motherboard's ports.

The easiest way to see is to hold the blanking plate up to the motherboard until the cutouts match the ports on your board. The blanking plate should be pushed against the motherboard with the ridge pointing out, so any text is readable. It will only fit one way, so manoeuvre it until it's the right way. Make a note of any ports that are covered.

3 REMOVE UNNECESSARY BITS
If you need to remove any parts of the blanking plate, you should do that now. You'll have two options for doing this. First, you may have to remove a bit of metal, in a similar way to the metal blanking plates on your case. These should be rocked gently out until the metal snaps.

Second, some ports may be covered by a flap. In this case, the flap should be bent inwards (towards where the motherboard will be). Make sure that you bend it far enough for the motherboard's port to be given enough clearance to pass underneath.

4 INSTALL THE BLANKING PLATE
From the inside of the case, you need to take the blanking plate and push it into the gap at

TIP
Motherboards can require a bit of force to be inserted. Push from the sides of the board; don't force any components, as you could damage them.

the rear of the case. Remember to align it so that it's the same way up as when you measured it against your motherboard.

The ridge round the outside of the plate should clip into the hole. Be warned that this can be really fiddly and the blanking plates don't always fit perfectly. It should, however, clip into place and remain stable without any support.

5 MEASURE WHERE THE MOTHERBOARD GOES

Next, you need to see where the screw holes for the motherboard will go. Lie the case flat on the desk and make sure that all the internal cables are out of the way. When you've got a clear case, take the motherboard off its foam backing and slide it gently into the case. Make sure that its rear ports are pushed up against the blanking plate correctly. Take a note of where the screw holes in the motherboard go, and remove the board. Place it back on its foam.

6 FIT THE RISERS

You need to fit risers where you noted the screw holes. These will be included with the case and look like tall copper screws. Their job is to hold the motherboard off the bottom of the case, so it isn't shorted out when its contacts touch the metal. The risers simply screw into the pre-drilled holes in

the case. Use as many risers as there are screw holes in the motherboard, making sure that you screw them tightly into position with your fingers.

7 SLIDE THE MOTHERBOARD INTO PLACE

Put the motherboard back in the case, making sure that all its screw holes have risers underneath. If some are missing, check to make sure that you haven't screwed the risers into the wrong place. You'll probably notice that the motherboard has a tendency to be slightly off from the risers. This is normal, and is caused by pressure from the backplate pushing against the motherboard. Simply line up the motherboard's ports with the backplate and push the motherboard towards it until the screw holes line up. This will take a bit of gentle force.

8 SCREW THE MOTHERBOARD DOWN

With the motherboard in place, you can start to screw it in. Start with the corners, holding the motherboard firmly, so that its screw holes line up with the risers that you put in.

When screwing the screws in, don't use too much pressure as you don't want to break the motherboard. Ideally, you want the screws tight enough for the board to be secure, but not so tight that it feels as though the board is going to start cracking.

Once you've done the corners, you can put screws in the other holes. How many you put in is up to you, but you shouldn't need to do all of them to make the motherboard secure. Keep going until the motherboard is firmly in place.

9 IDENTIFY ATX CONNECTORS
With the motherboard in place, you're ready to connect it to the power supply. There are two connectors that you'll need to plug in. The first is the ATX connector. On modern motherboards, you need a 24-pin connector. There's only one of these on the power supply. However, as older motherboards only required a 20-pin connector, there's usually a four-pin connector that can be detached. Make sure that this is connected and that you have an unbroken 24-pin connector.

10 PLUG IN ATX CONNECTOR
You need to plug this 24-pin connector into the matching connector on the motherboard. This should be easy to find, but it's usually located by the IDE ports on the right-hand side of the motherboard.

The ATX connector will only plug in one way, so you can't get it wrong. Once it's lined up, the connector should plug in smoothly. There's a clip on it to hold it in place. This will require gentle pressure to get it to clip in, but no more. If you're

having to force the cable, then the chances are that you've got the connector the wrong way round. Once the cable is in place, give it a gentle tug to make sure that it's secure.

11 IDENTIFY SECONDARY CONNECTOR
Modern motherboards also have a secondary power connector. On most boards this is a single four-pin connector, but some require eight-pin connectors. Check to see what your power supply has, as you may need to buy an adaptor.

In a similar way to the 24-pin connector, the eight-pin connector on power supplies can be split into two. If your motherboard has only a four-pin connector, you'll have to split it into two halves. Only one of these will plug into the motherboard.

12 CONNECT SECONDARY CONNECTOR
Locate the secondary motherboard power connector. Your board's manual will tell you exactly where it's located, but on most motherboards it's near the processor socket. Next, plug the power supply's secondary connector into it. This plug will only go in one way, so there's no chance of getting it wrong. The connector should slide gently into the plug. You'll need to apply a bit of force in order to get the clip to lock into place, and you should hear it click when it's in properly.

TIP
Make sure that the power connectors are connected properly by giving them a gentle tug.

GIGABYTE™

Leader in Motherboard Innovation

From Ultra Durable III to Super IV

4 Phase⁺ Power Design 3x USB Power Boost

GIGABYTE has further improved on the CPU VRM area by increasing the power phases from 3 to 4 phase design at least. This allows for more stable power delivery to the CPU, as well as help smooth out power ripple and noise which is important for clean CPU power delivery.

GIGABYTE	GIGABYTE
150W	2A
Others 90W	Others 0.5A
CPU Power Support	USB Port Power

GIGABYTE motherboards feature a 3x USB power boost, delivering greater compatibility and extra power for USB devices. GIGABYTE's unique USB power design is also able to efficiently regulate output over the full voltage range, which greatly enhances USB device compatibility. In addition, dedicated lower resistance fuses ensure lower voltage drops, and provide more stable and plentiful power delivery.

108dB Signal-to-Noise ratio playback

GIGABYTE strongly believes that in 2011, HD audio playback is a standard specification, and as such, we have made Blu-ray audio playback a standard for all of our motherboards.

All of GIGABYTE's 2011 motherboards feature higher capability audio solution with 108dB Signal-to-Noise ratio (SNR) playback quality to deliver high-performance, multi-channel HD audio. SNR is a comparison of the amount of signal to the amount of noise such as hiss present in the signal (expressed in Decibels). A higher SNR equals a better audio experience. For example, 108dB, is a high audio specification, as this means the audio signal is 108dB higher than the level of the noise.

Long-Life Spec

GIGABYTE was the first motherboard manufacturer to realize the importance of using only the highest quality components for the critically important CPU VRM zone of the motherboard which is responsible for delivering stable power to the CPU. The GIGABYTE Ultra Durable™ 2 design utilizes All Solid Capacitors manufactured in Japan which are rated to last for at least 50,000 hours in operational use. GIGABYTE Ultra Durable™ 2 motherboards also feature Ferrite Core Chokes with higher energy efficiency compared to more common iron core chokes and Lower RDS(on) MOSFETs which feature lower resistance, i.e. reduced power consumption and heat. Some motherboards in this segment feature the GIGABYTE Ultra Durable™ 2 Classic design, which features All Solid Japanese manufactured Capacitors and Lower RDS(on) MOSFETs.

DualBIOS™ 3TB+ HDD Support (Hybrid EFI Technology)

Hybrid EFI Technology combines the benefits of GIGABYTE's mature BIOS platform including stability and compatibility with 3rd party products with 3TB+ HDD support from EFI technology, allowing GIGABYTE to offer the best of both worlds through a quick and easy BIOS update using GIGABYTE's @BIOS utility that is freely available from the GIGABYTE website.

GIGABYTE DualBIOS™ is a patented technology that automatically recovers BIOS data when the main BIOS has crashed or failed. Featuring 2 physical BIOS ROMs integrated onboard, GIGABYTE DualBIOS™ allows quick and seamless recovery from BIOS damage or failure due to viruses or improper BIOS updating. In addition, GIGABYTE DualBIOS™ now supports 3TB+ (terabyte) hard drive booting without the need for partitioning, and enables more data storage on a single hard drive.

GA-Z68X-UD7-B3

Winner of the PC Pro motherboard excellence award **5 years** in a row, Voted for by PC Pro readers

HOW TO...
Install an Intel processor

1 LIFT THE PROCESSOR CAGE
Intel's processor sockets are covered by a cage. A new motherboard will also have a plastic cover on top. First, remove this cover. It should easily unclip. To access the socket, unclip the handle that runs down the side of the socket and lift it up. This releases the retaining clip for the main cage.

Lift the main cage up and out of the way to expose the socket. Be careful not to touch any of the pins inside the socket, as bending them will stop the processor from working correctly.

2 INSTALL THE PROCESSOR
The processor has two cut-out notches in its sides, which line up with the ridges in the socket. This prevents the processor from being put in the wrong way round. You'll also notice an arrow on the processor. This should line up with the corner of the socket that has its pins arranged diagonally.

Line the processor up and sit it gently in the place. If it doesn't sit properly, then you've got it the wrong way round. Once you're happy with the processor's position, close the drive cage and pull the retaining handle down. This should take a bit of force, but if it feels like there's too much resistance, check that the processor is seated properly.

3 APPLY THERMAL PASTE
Thermal paste fills in micro-cracks in the surface of the processor and the surface of the cooler, ensuring that there's efficient heat transfer between the two. Some fans come pre-coated with thermal paste, in which case you can skip this step.

If yours doesn't, you'll need to apply your own. This is easy to do. First, squeeze a tiny blob of thermal paste into the middle of the processor. Take a thin bit of card and use this to spread it, so that the surface of the processor is coated. Don't spread it over the side of the cage, and add more thermal paste if you don't have enough.

4 ATTACH THE FAN
Most Intel coolers clip into the four round holes on the outside of the processor socket. If you're not using an Intel reference cooler bundled with your processor, check the cooler's instructions; some need a backplate screwed to the motherboard.

For all other coolers, you'll see four feet. Make sure that all the feet are rotated away from the direction of the arrow. Line up the cooler so that

TIP
The plastic clips on Intel coolers can be annoying to fit. Make sure the black plastic clips are raised before fitting the cooler, and push diagonally opposite clips in together.

the four feet touch the holes in the motherboard. It's best to try to get the power cable pointing towards the header on the motherboard marked CPU (we'll cover this later).

Starting at diagonally opposite sides, push the four feet into the place. You'll need some force, and the feet should click into position. When done, check the cooler is seated properly and that it isn't wobbly. If it is, make sure the feet are properly in position.

HOW TO...
Install an AMD processor

1 OPEN THE SOCKET LEVER

AMD's processors fit into AM2, AM2+ or AM3 sockets. The sockets are very similar, so the installation instructions are the same.

To fit the processor in the socket, first lift the lever. This unclips to one side and rises vertically above the board. This will move the socket very slightly, aligning the holes in the plastic socket with the connectors beneath. The processor should drop into place with no force, hence the socket's type: zero insertion force (ZIF).

2 FIT THE PROCESSOR

The processor can fit only one way into the socket. Make sure the arrow on top of the processor is aligned with the arrow on the processor socket. Gently push the processor into place. You should feel it click into position when it's all the way in. If it feels like you have to use too much force, stop and check that the processor is correctly aligned.

Once the processor is all the way in, check round it to make sure that it's sitting flush against the plastic socket. If it's not, push gently down on the sections that aren't flush. Push the lever down and clip it back into place to secure the processor.

3 APPLY THERMAL PASTE

Thermal paste fills in micro-cracks in the surface of the processor and the surface of the cooler, ensuring that there's efficient heat transfer between the two. You may find that your fan comes pre-coated with thermal paste, in which case you can skip this step.

If not, you'll need to apply your own. This is simple to do. First, squeeze a tiny blob of thermal paste into the middle of the processor. Take a thin bit of card and use this to spread it, so that the surface of the processor is coated. Don't spread it over the side of the processor, and add more thermal paste if necessary.

4 FIT THE COOLER

If you're using a third-party cooler, check its instructions for how to fit it. If you're using an AMD cooler that came with your processor, fitting it is simple. Around the processor socket is a plastic cooler mount, with two nodules sticking out. These are designed to hold your cooler's clips.

Take your cooler and open its handle. Fit the metal clip without the handle on it over one nodule and push it snugly against the mount. Place the cooler flat across the top of the processor. Push the cooler's remaining metal clip over the second nodule and close the handle. This will require a bit of force to get the handle all the way down. We'll cover connecting the fan's power connector later.

TIP
If you bend the pins on your AMD processor, slide a credit card into the row of bent pins to straighten them.

Installing memory

DUAL MEMORY Motherboards have dual memory channels. Installing two memory modules – one in each channel – can increase performance. The slots to use are usually the same colour, but check your motherboard's

NOTCH The notch in the middle of the memory slot prevents the wrong type of memory from being installed.

CLIPS The clips at the side of the memory slot hold the RAM in place. You open them to install memory, and they close automatically when the RAM is installed.

HOW TO...
Install memory

1 IDENTIFY WHICH SLOTS TO USE
Presuming that you've bought memory in a kit with two sticks of RAM, you should now identify the slots in which you're going to install the memory. As noted opposite, the slots to use are usually the same colour, but you should check your motherboard's manual carefully to make sure that you're using the right ones.

To be doubly safe, the slots will also be numbered to make it easier to follow the motherboard manual's instructions.

2 OPEN THE RETAINING CLIPS
To install your memory, you need to open the clips on either end of the slot into which you're going to insert your memory stick. Pick the first slot and push open these clips; they should open gently without any force, clicking as they open. The clips should open to around 45°, but don't force them further open when you feel resistance.

3 LINE THE MEMORY UP
To fit the memory, you need to slide it into the slot. Make sure that the notch in the memory lines up with the ridge in the socket. If it doesn't, then you've got the memory the wrong way round.

If the memory still doesn't fit, then you're using the wrong type of memory. Check the memory's instructions and motherboard's manual to see what type you need.

4 CLIP THE MEMORY INTO PLACE
Once the memory module is lined up, press firmly on both sides to push it into place. The clips should spring back and click into position. Check the clips are in place and nestled against the notches in the side of the memory module. If they're not, try pushing the memory down a bit further. You can also push the clips up to help them lock into place.

Once your first module is in place, repeat these steps for any remaining modules.

TIP
Push down evenly on both sides of the module, or you'll find it hard to get the retaining clips to lock into place.

HOW TO...
Fit the internal cables

1 POWER

To get your PC to turn on when you push the power button, you need to connect the power switch to the motherboard. Among the loose cables in your case, you'll find a two-pin connector. This will usually be marked PWR SW, but check the case's manual if you're not sure.

This needs to be connected to the power jumpers on the motherboard. Typically, these will be located on the bottom-right of the motherboard and will be marked, although you should double-check your motherboard's manual to make sure. The connector will just plug over the two pins and should connect easily.

2 RESET

If your case has a reset switch – not all do – then there will be a similar connector to the power switch, with RESET SW written on it. Connecting this to your motherboard lets you restart your PC after a major crash, as it resets the hardware and forces your computer to reboot.

To connect it, you need to find the reset jumpers on the motherboard. These will be near the power switch, but you should read your motherboard's manual for an exact location. Simply push the connector over the two pins

to connect the switch. It doesn't matter which way round this connector goes.

3 POWER AND HDD LEDS

The HDD connector connects to an LED on the front of the case and lights up when the hard disk is in operation. This is useful, as you can see whether your PC's working or if it's crashed.

As this connects to an LED, it must be connected correctly. The cable should be marked as positive and negative (this is usually written on the plug). The motherboard HDD jumper will also have a positive and negative port. Check your motherboard's manual carefully to make sure you get this right, and then connect the cable.

Do the same thing for the power LED, which will have a similar connector. This must be connected the right way round, so make sure you get the positive and negative connectors aligned.

4 USB

If your case has front-mounted USB ports or a card reader, you'll need to connect these to spare headers on your motherboard. In all likelihood, the cable in the case will be marked USB.

Your motherboard will probably have spare connectors marked USB, but the manual can tell you exactly where these are. USB connectors take power, so you need to plug the cable in the right way round. Fortunately, the USB ports on most cases have a single plug that can only be connected to the motherboard in one way. If it doesn't, you'll need to check the case's and motherboard's manuals carefully to make sure that you install the connectors correctly.

Assuming you're using a block connector, plug it into a spare USB header on the motherboard. We'd recommend using the closest header to the cable to avoid draping cables everywhere.

5 FIREWIRE
Front-mounted FireWire cables plug in much the same way as USB cables. Again, look for a spare FireWire header on the motherboard (the manual will explain where these are), and then connect the FireWire cable to it. The cable may be marked as 1394, as FireWire is also known as i1394.

6 AUDIO
Front-mounted audio ports also need to be connected to the motherboard if you want to be able to plug in your headphones and a microphone. Fortunately, most motherboards and cases have a single block connector that plugs into the front audio connector on the motherboard.

Your motherboard's manual will have full details of where this is connected, but it's usually located by its back panel. Again, there's only one way to connect this cable, so just slide it gently into place. If your case has a Speaker header, plug this into

the appropriate connector on the motherboard. This is used to give warning beeps.

7 FANS
It's common for modern cases to have extra fans pre-fitted. These help increase airflow through the case and keep your PC cool. While fans can be connected directly to the power supply, it's better to connect them to spare fan headers on the motherboard. This way, the motherboard can automatically control the fan speed and keep your PC running as quietly as possible.

If your fans end in three- or four-pin connectors, you can plug them into your motherboard. Look at the manual to find a spare fan connector and then plug in the fan's power connector. Three-pin connectors can plug into four-pin ports and vice versa. The cables can also plug in only one way, so it's easy to get it right.

8 CPU FAN
The processor fan, which we installed earlier, can now be connected to the motherboard. In the same way as system fans, the processor's fan speed is controlled by the motherboard based on the processor's temperature. This keeps your computer as quiet as possible.

There's a special connector for the processor fan on the motherboard, which is often called CPU FAN. Check your motherboard's manual for its location. This is likely to be a four-pin connector, but three-pin processor fans can also plug in. The connector can go in only one way, so just plug it in.

TIP

LED connectors need to be connected the right way round, or you'll break the light.

Installing a hard disk

SATA POWER Plug the hard disk's power in here.

SATA DATA Plug one end of the data cable in here and the other end into a SATA port on the motherboard.

TIP
If you're installing more than one hard disk, plug the one from which you want to boot in the lowest-numbered SATA port. The BIOS will pick this hard disk as the boot drive by default.

SATA PORTS These are for hard disks, newer DVD writers and Blu-ray drives. SATA3 ports, if available, are for hard disks and SSDs.

HOW TO...
Install a hard disk

1 FIT HARD DISK INTO A BAY

To fit a hard disk, you'll need a spare 3½in drive bay. Be careful not to use one of the external bays, which have a cutout on the front of the case, as these are designed for memory card readers and floppy disk drives.

If your case has drive rails or screwless fittings, you'll need to read the case's manual for instructions on how to fit a drive. For other cases, slide the hard disk into a spare drive bay until the screw holes in the side of the drive line up with the holes in the drive bay. The disk should then be secured with four screws, two on either side. Suitable screws should have been provided with the hard disk or case. Screw them tightly to prevent the drive wobbling.

2 PLUG IN SATA POWER

In the main picture opposite, you can see the SATA power connector on the hard disk and on the power supply. Locate the correct connector from your power supply and plug it into the back of your hard disk. It goes in only one way and clicks when it's connected. Be extremely careful when plugging it in, as downwards pressure can break the clip surrounding the power connector. If this happens, the power plug won't stay in place.

3 PLUG IN SATA DATA CABLE

Unlike IDE, SATA uses a simple and thin connector to carry data. Your motherboard will ship with several SATA cables, so take one of these from the box. Plug it gently into the rear of the hard disk. It will plug in only one way and will click when it's properly connected.

Be careful when you plug it in, as downwards pressure can break the connector and prevent the SATA cable plugging in.

4 PLUG SATA DATA CABLE INTO MOTHERBOARD

Next, you need to find a spare SATA port on your motherboard. These are usually located at the bottom-right of the board and are numbered. The lower the number, the higher up the boot chain your hard disk is. If you're installing more than one hard disk, therefore, make sure the drive from which you're going to boot is plugged into the lowest-numbered port. Check the motherboard's manual to ensure that all the ports do the same thing; some boards have ports reserved for RAID.

Connecting the SATA cable is easy, as it will plug in only one way. It will click when the cable is connected properly.

TIP
SATA connectors on hard disks can be broken easily, so be careful when inserting and moving cables.

Installing an SSD

SATA POWER Plug the SSD's power in here.

SATA DATA Plug one end of the data cable in here and the other end into a SATA port on the motherboard.

TIP Make sure that your SSD is plugged into the lowest-numbered SATA port in order for it to be the default boot drive. If available, a SATA3 port should be used for the best performance.

SATA PORTS These are for hard disks, newer DVD writers and Blu-ray drives. SATA3 ports, if available, are for SSDs.

HOW TO...
Install an SSD

1 FIT SSD INTO BAY

Most solid-state drives (SSDs) are designed to fit in a 2½in laptop drive bay, which you won't find in a PC. Fortunately, they come with mounting brackets to get them to fit, so screw these in before you start. Next, find a 3½in drive bay. Be careful not to use an external bay, which have a cutout on the front of the case, as these are for memory card readers and floppy disk drives.

If your case has drive rails or screwless fittings, read the case's manual for instructions on how to fit your drive. For other cases, slide the hard disk into a spare drive bay until the screw holes in the side of the drive line up with the holes in the drive bay. The disk should then be secured with four screws, two on either side of the case.

2 PLUG IN SATA POWER

In the main picture opposite, you can see the SATA power connector on the hard disk and on the power supply. Locate the correct connector from your power supply and plug it into the back of your SSD. It goes in only one way and clicks when it's connected. Be extremely careful when plugging it in, as downwards pressure can break the clip surrounding the power connector. If you do this, the power plug won't stay in place.

3 PLUG IN SATA DATA CABLE

Unlike IDE, SATA uses a simple and thin connector to carry data. Your motherboard will ship with several SATA cables, so take one of these from the box. Plug it gently into the rear of the SSD. It will plug in only one way and will click when it's properly connected.

Be careful when you plug it in, as downwards pressure can break the connector and prevent the SATA cable plugging in.

4 PLUG SATA DATA CABLE INTO MOTHERBOARD

Next, you need to find a spare SATA port on your motherboard. These are usually located at the bottom-right of the board and are numbered. The lower the number, the higher up the boot chain your SSD is. If you're installing more than one hard disk, therefore, make sure the drive from which you're going to boot is plugged into the lowest-numbered port. Check the motherboard's manual to ensure that all the ports do the same thing; some boards have ports reserved for RAID.

Connecting the SATA cable is easy, as it will plug in only one way. It will click when the cable is connected properly.

TIP
Find out how to configure Windows for your SSD, see page 96

Installing an optical drive

SATA POWER Plug the hard disk's power in here.

SATA DATA Plug one end of the data cable in here and the other end into into a SATA port on the motherboard.

TIP If you're installing more than one IDE drive, you'll need to set the jumpers on the rear so that one drive is the master and the other is the slave.

JUMPER Use this to set the drive to Master or Slave.

IDE CONNECTOR Plug the IDE data cable in here.

POWER CONNECTOR Plug a Molex power connector in here.

HOW TO...
Connect an optical drive

1 FIT THE DRIVE

First, fit the optical drive into a spare 5¼in drive bay in the case. Some cases have flaps at the front to hide the optical drive from view. If you have a screwless case or your drives need to be fitted on runners, consult your case's manual for full instructions.

Other cases require you to screw the drive into place. The optical drive needs to be slid into the case from the front. This often means that you need to have the front of the case removed, if you haven't done that yet. Slide the drive into the bay. The front of it needs to be flush with the case where there's no flap, and slightly further back if your case has a drive flap.

To tell where the drive should be, push it in until the screw holes in its side match up with the round screw holes inside the case. Now use the four screws (provided with the optical drive or case) – two either side – to hold the drive in place.

2 FIT THE IDE CABLE

Most optical drives use the older IDE data connector. If yours uses SATA, follow the instructions for fitting a hard disk (page 62). An IDE cable is a wide ribbon cable. It's harder to plug in than a SATA cable, but shouldn't cause any problems if you know what to look out for. First, the cable can plug in only one way due to a blocked-off connector in the cable. Second, the coloured cable (red or white depending on the cable provided with your motherboard) goes to the right of the connector closest to the power connector. Plug the cable in gently and as straight as possible so as not to bend any pins on the drive.

3 FIT THE POWER CABLE

Optical drives tend to use a Molex power connector. This is the large four-pin connector on your power supply. Locate a free one and push it into the drive's power connector. Use a bit of force to get it to connect properly. Once you think it's in, give it a gentle tug to make sure it's secure.

4 FIT THE IDE CABLE INTO THE MOTHERBOARD

Now you're ready to plug the cable into the motherboard. Be careful not to get the connector confused with the floppy disk connector; check your motherboard's manual for its location. The IDE connector can plug in only one way, thanks to a notch in the motherboard's connector. Plug in the cable gently as straight as possible to avoid bending any pins.

TIP If your IDE cable doesn't have a notch in it, face the red cable towards the power connector on the drive.

Installing a graphics card

CROSSFIRE CONNECTOR This is used when you install two ATI graphics cards. Nvidia cards have a similar SLI connector.

PCI EXPRESS x16 CONNECTOR This plugs into the corresponding slot on the motherboard.

PCI EXPRESS POWER CONNECTOR Connect your power supply's graphics power connector in here.

TIP
PCI Express x16 slots typically have retaining clips. You'll need to use this clip if you have to remove a graphics card later.

HOW TO...
Install a graphics card

1 REMOVE BLANKING PLATE
First, locate the PCI Express x16 slot and remove the associated blanking plate. If you're going to be fitting a double-height card, then you'll need to remove the blanking plate on the next expansion slot as well.

The procedure will differ depending on your case, so check its manual for full details. Typically, blanking plates are either screwed in place individually, or they're all held in place by a single retaining bar. Some blanking plates just lift out, while others are attached to the case and need to be rocked backwards and forwards to snap them out.

2 PLUG CARD INTO SLOT
With the blanking plates free, you can put your card into the case. This is easy to do: simply line up the graphics card's connector with the slot in the case. The card should look like it's upside down, with the fan pointing towards the bottom of the case.

Pressure on both sides of the card should be enough to make sure that it ends up seated in the expansion card slot properly. You should check the card when you think it's in place to ensure that you've made proper contact. If you can still see some of the card's slot sticking out, then push the relevant side in a bit further.

3 SCREW CARD IN PLACE
How you remove the blanking plate will depend on how you attach your card securely, so check the case's manual for full details. In most instances, you'll need to screw the card into place. Line up the top of its connector with the screw hole in the case and screw it into place so that the card can't move in its slot.

4 CONNECT POWER ADAPTOR
Most modern graphics cards require a secondary power source to run. These will need a dedicated PCI Express six-pin power connector. Most modern power supplies have one of these, but if yours doesn't, a Molex-to-PCI Express adaptor is often bundled with graphics cards. The PCI Express power connector can plug in only one way and can be pushed easily into place.

TIP
Don't forget to plug in the PCI Express power connector, if required, or your PC may not turn on.

ASUS *DirectCU II* Dual Fan Graphics Cards
RAGING COOL

ASUS DirectCU II uses copper heat pipes in direct contact with the GPU core, delivering up to 20% cooler performance. DirectCU II adds a custom cooler that uses twin 100mm fans for a massive 600% increase in airflow on HD6970 and GTX580 DirectCU II cards.

600% Greater Air Flow

20% Cooler than Reference!

ENGTX580 DCII/2DIS/1536MD5

- DirectX 11 Ready
- NVIDIA PhysX Ready
- Shader Clock 1544MHZ
- NVIDIA 3D Vision Ready
- Video Memory 1536MB GDDR5
- Engine Clock 782Mhz Factory Overclocked
- GeForce CUDA Support, CUDA Cores 512
- Memory Clock 4008MHz (1002MHz GDDR5)

EAH6970 DCII/2DI4S/2GD5

- DirectX 11Ready
- Engine Clock 890MHz
- AMD 3D Technology
- Memory Clock 890MHz
- AMD Eyefinity Technology
- Video Memory GDDR5 2GB
- AMD CrossFire Technology

DirectCU II graphics cards include exclusive ASUS Super Alloy Power Technology. This uses a unique alloy formula in power components such as chokes, capacitors, POSCAPs and MOSFETS delivering:

- Up to a 15% Performance Boost
- 35°C Cooler Operation
- 2.5 x Longer Life Span

ASUS Voltage Tweak Utility allows gamers to realise the full performance potential from their graphics card with an intuitive user interface.

Installing expansion cards

PCI SLOTS An older type of expansion slot, but plenty of cards will still fit them.

PCI EXPRESS x1 SLOT The newest type of expansion slot. Also look out for x4 slots, which look similar but are longer.

TIP PCI Express cards can fit in higher socket types, so an x1 card can fit in an x4 slot, for example, and an x4 card fits in an x16 slot.

PCI EXPRESS x16 SLOTS If you don't install a dedicated graphics card, these slots can be used for expansion cards.

HOW TO...
Plug in expansion cards

1 LOCATE SPARE SLOT

Before you start, carefully read the instructions that came with your expansion card as some require you to install software first. If yours does, you'll need to finish building the PC and install the operating system and necessary software before fitting the expansion card.

When you're ready, find a spare PCI or PCI Express slot on your motherboard. Ideally, leave a gap between other expansion cards, such as your graphics card, to increase airflow and keep your PC running cool.

2 REMOVE BLANKING PLATE

To fit an expansion card, you'll need to remove the expansion slot's blanking plate. The procedure will differ depending on your case, so carefully check its manual for full details. Typically, blanking plates are either individually screwed in place or held in place by a single retaining bar. Remove whatever's holding the blanking plates in place. Some plates just lift out, while others are attached to the case and need to be rocked backwards and forwards to snap them out.

3 FIT THE CARD

PCI and PCI Express cards are fitted in the same way. Line up the connector on the bottom of the card with the slot in which you want to put it. Slots have notches part of the way along, which you need to line up with the gap in the card's connector. When you've done this, push the card into place. It will take a bit of force to get the card to slide home properly. If the card doesn't feel like it's going to go into the slot, remove it and make sure it's lined up and that you're trying to install it into the correct slot. When the card is in place, check round it to make sure the connector is firmly in the slot. If the card doesn't look level, apply pressure to the part of the card sticking up until it clicks into place.

4 SCREW IT IN

When your card is firmly in place, you need to secure it in its slot. As some cases use proprietary fixing methods, check your case's manual for instructions on how to do this. If you need to use a screw, line up the screw hole in the card's blanking plate with the screw hole in the case. Tighten the screw up to the point where the card feels firm and doesn't wobble in the slot.

TIP
Try to use alternate slots in order to improve airflow and stop adjacent cards from heating one another up.

GIGABYTE™
Leader in Motherboard Innovation

GIGABYTE
Z68AP-D3 Motherboard

Only £79.99*

- Supports Latest i3/i5/i7 LGA1155 CPU
- Latest Intel Z68 Express Chipset
- 4x DDR3 Dimm Slots supporting upto 32 GB System Memory
- Dual Channel Memory Architecture
- 2x SATA 6GB/s 3x SATA 3GB/s Ports
- 2x USB 3.0 Ports – Up to 10 USB 2.0 Ports
- Supports HDMI Output up to 1920 x 1200 1080P Resolution
- 3 Year Warranty

Box Gaming Bundles
Powered by Gigabyte

Only £449*

- Gigabyte Z68AP-D3 Motherboard
- Gainward GTX 560 TI 1GB DDR5 Video Card
- Intel Core i5 2500k CPU
- Kingston Hyper X Memory 4GB Kit 1600Mhz
- Free Batman Arkham City Game with Video Card

Only £699*

- Gigabyte Z68AP-D3 Motherboard
- Gainward GTX 560 TI 1Gb DDR Golden Sample Video Card. Winner of premium grade Custom PC!
- Intel Core i7 2600k CPU + Coolermaster TX3 Cooler
- Kingston Hyper X Memory 8Gb 1600Mhz (4x 2GB)
- Coolermaster Silencio 550 Tower Gaming Case
- Coolermaster GX650 650W Power Supply
- Free Batman Arkham City Game with Video Card

Order securely online: www.box.co.uk
or visit our Birmingham store

📞 **0121 202 0030** 10am - 6pm Mon - Fri

HOW TO...
Put the case back together

1 TIDY THE CABLES

If the inside of your computer is neat and tidy, you'll get better airflow and keep it cooler. A neat PC is also easier to work on should you need to install an upgrade later on.

One way to keep your case tidy is to fit cable ties. Simply locate loose cables that are running in the same direction and loop a cable tie around the bunch. Slide the strap through the buckle and pull it tight. The ratchet should click into place and stop the cable becoming undone. If it doesn't, you've inserted the strap the wrong way into the buckle. You can clip the long strap off when you're done. For extra neatness, loop the strap through drive bays in the case. This will anchor your cables out of the way.

2 KEEP CABLES OUT OF FANS

It's worth double-checking that none of your power cables is in the way of the fans inside your PC. If they are, you run the risk of severing your cables when you turn your PC on for the first time. Pull any loose cables out of the way of fans and secure them with cable ties if necessary. The processor fan (particularly on Intel's designs) is often the worse culprit for snagging cables, so check this one carefully.

3 ATTACH FRONT

Check your case's manual for the exact fitting instructions. If you removed its front, now is the time to fit it again. Line its clips up with the holes in the case and push firmly to reattach it. If you find that your optical drive sticks out too far, you've probably fitted it incorrectly. Undo its screws (or fixings if your case is screwless) and slide it further into the case. Screw it back in and fit the front of the case.

4 ATTACH SIDES

Check your case's manual carefully for full fitting instructions. For most cases, fitting the side panels is a matter of lining up their clips with the grooves on the inside of the case. Take each panel in turn, slide it into place and attach it firmly with a screw.

BUILDING YOUR PC

5 CONNECT NETWORK CABLE

If you want to connect your PC to a broadband router via an Ethernet cable, now's the time to plug it in. Windows 7 and Vista can use the internet to search for updated drivers, to make your installation smoother. Even if you're not using Windows 7 or Vista, being able to connect straight to the internet after installing an operating system is really useful.

6 CONNECT KEYBOARD AND MOUSE

To install an operating system, you'll need to connect a mouse and keyboard. Most motherboards support older PS2 keyboards and mice as well as newer USB models. PS2 keyboards plug into the purple port and mice into the green one. Simply line up the notch in the plug with the one in the port in the back of your computer and push.

For USB keyboards and mice, plug the connector into a free USB port; it will go only one way. For other USB devices, check their manuals before plugging them in. Many devices require you to install drivers first, so you'll have to install the operating system before you can plug them in.

7 CONNECT SPEAKERS

You can connect your speakers to your PC now. This is useful, as after installing an operating system you'll be able to check instantly whether

the sound is working properly. How you connect your speakers will depend on how many you're plugging in. Generally speaking, surround-sound speakers have colour-coded cables, so you just need to match the cable with the same-coloured port on the back of your PC. For stereo speakers, plug a 3½mm jack into the green port on the back of the PC. Headphones generally connect to the green port on the front of the case.

8 PLUG IN MONITOR

Finally, you need to connect your computer to a monitor. This is simple. If your screen has a DVI input and your graphics card has a DVI output (pictured), you need a DVI-to-DVI cable. These are D-shaped, so they will plug in only one way. Line up the cable with the graphics card's connector and push the cable straight in. Screw it in place using the thumbscrews on either side of the connector. Repeat this on job on the monitor.

If your monitor has a blue analogue D-sub connector, you have two options. For graphics cards with DVI outputs, you'll have to plug in a DVI-to-D-sub connector first. You can then plug the D-sub cable into this and the monitor. If you're using onboard graphics with a D-sub output, plug the cable directly into this and the monitor. Just like DVI connectors, D-sub connectors are D-shaped, so they'll plug in only one way.

TIP

DVI-to-VGA adaptors will let you plug in an analogue monitor if you have only DVI outputs.

CMOS Setup Utility - Copyri
MB Intellig

System Memory Multiplier (SPD)
Memory Frequency(Mhz)   800
DRAM Timing Selectable   (SPD)
******** Standard Timing Contr
CAS Latency Time   5
DRAM RAS# to CAS# Delay   5
DRAM RAS# Precharge   5
Precharge delay(tRAS)   18
******** Advanced Timing Contr
ACT to ACT Delay(tRRD)   3
Rank Write To READ Delay   3
Write To Precharge Delay   6
Refresh to ACT Delay   42
Read to Precharge Delay
Static tRead Value
Static tRead Phase Adjust
Command Rate(CMD)
****** Clock Driving & Skew
CPU/PCIEX Clock Driving Cont

↑↓→←:Move   Enter:Select   +/-/PU
    F5:Previous Values   F6:Fai

BEFORE YOU CAN install an operating
system on your newly assembled PC,
you'll need to change a few settings in
the BIOS. The BIOS – or basic input/
output system – is where you can
configure the speed of your processor
and memory, alter settings such as the
system password and choose when
your PC boots up every day.
In this chapter, we'll show you how to
access the BIOS and make the
appropriate changes.

IN THIS CHAPTER

Into the BIOS   80

Into the BIOS

THE BASIC INPUT/OUTPUT SYSTEM (BIOS) is the part of your motherboard that detects and controls all your PC's hardware. It's been replaced on new motherboards with the United Extensible Firmware Interface (UEFI), which is very similar to the BIOS but is more graphical and can be controlled with a mouse. The menus and steps for configuring the UEFI are otherwise the same as depicted here, though.

Your BIOS makes sure that all your hardware is working correctly before your operating system starts. Getting it configured correctly will make your PC run more smoothly and reduce the number of errors you see. It's important to check the BIOS settings when you buy a new

motherboard, perform an upgrade, or have to replace the onboard battery.

The BIOS can be a confusing place to visit, so in this chapter we'll show you how to configure it.

ENTERING THE BIOS
The first thing you have to do is get into the BIOS. You do this by pressing a hotkey when you first turn on your PC. Typically, you need to press the Delete key when you first see something on your computer's display. However, we've seen some BIOSes that use F1, F2 or F10. Look out for an onscreen message that tells you which key to press. If you press the key too late, press Ctrl-Alt-Del to restart your computer.

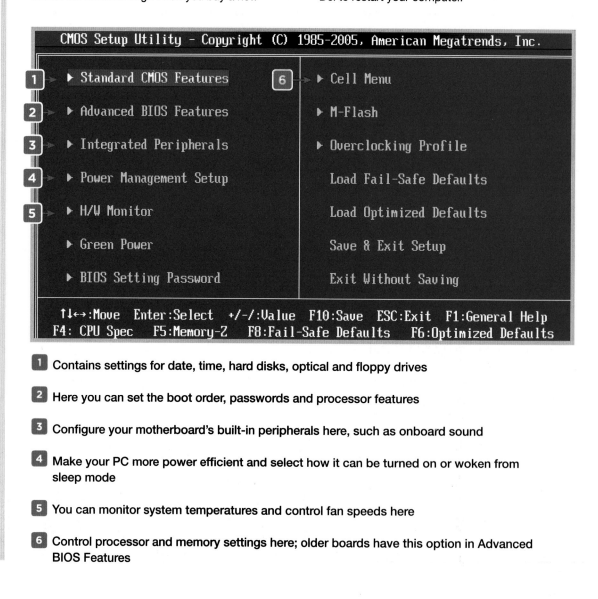

1 Contains settings for date, time, hard disks, optical and floppy drives

2 Here you can set the boot order, passwords and processor features

3 Configure your motherboard's built-in peripherals here, such as onboard sound

4 Make your PC more power efficient and select how it can be turned on or woken from sleep mode

5 You can monitor system temperatures and control fan speeds here

6 Control processor and memory settings here; older boards have this option in Advanced BIOS Features

```
CMOS Setup Utility - Copyright (C) 1985-2005, American Megatrends, Inc.
                        Standard CMOS Features

  Date(MM:DD:YY) :      [Wed 10/14/2009]        Help Item
  Time(HH:MM:SS) :      [05:43:53]

  ▶ IDE Primary Master   [Not Detected]
  ▶ IDE Primary Slave    [Not Detected]
  ▶ E-SATA1              [Not Detected]
  ▶ E-SATA2              [Not Detected]

  Floppy Drive A         [Not Installed]
  Hold On                [All Error]

  ▶ System Information    [Press Enter]




  ↑↓←→:Move  Enter:Select  +/-/:Value  F10:Save  ESC:Exit  F1:General Help
  F4: CPU Spec   F5:Memory-Z   F8:Fail-Safe Defaults   F6:Optimized Defaults
```

↑ The Standard CMOS Features page lets you set your PC's date and time

Once you're inside the BIOS, you'll see a set of menus. The screenshot opposite shows you what each option is for. Your PC's BIOS may not look exactly like this, as each one is slightly different. However, this screenshot is representative of most BIOSes, and the options we'll tell you to change will be available on the vast majority of computers, although you may need to hunt for them a bit.

One word of warning: changing settings that you don't understand can damage your PC. We recommend following our instructions carefully; you should make changes to other settings only if you're confident of what you're doing. We'll walk you through the settings that you should check in your BIOS in order. Navigate through the BIOS using your computer's cursor keys and select a menu option by pressing Enter. You can press Escape to move back a menu.

SETTING THE DATE AND TIME

First, select the Standard CMOS Features menu. The next screen will show you your computer's date and time. Set them correctly, as a wrong date and time can prevent things such as secure websites from working properly, as your PC can think that a website's identification certificate is out of date. If your time was set correctly but keeps resetting itself, you'll need to replace your motherboard's CMOS battery.

To set the date and time, select the day, month and year individually, pressing '+' or '-' to increase or decrease the value. This screen may also display your hard disks and optical drives, depending on your computer's storage

configuration. At the very least, it will display all IDE devices connected to your computer, but not necessarily SATA devices.

The final options let you select whether you have a floppy disk drive and how to handle errors. If you don't have a floppy drive, select Not Installed from the menu. It's best to set the computer to Hold On All Errors: if you have a problem, this will stop your computer from booting Windows, which could potentially cause even more problems.

ADVANCED STORAGE SETTINGS

Press Esc to go back to the main menu and then select Integrated Peripherals. Look for a menu called On-Chip ATA Devices or similar. There may be an option for SATA devices in the Integrate Peripherals menu. Here you should be able to change the SATA mode (it may also be called RAID mode). Select it and you'll have a choice of options: IDE, RAID and AHCI.

IDE makes your SATA hard disks act like older IDE hard disks, while RAID lets you use multiple hard disks to create one logical drive with either built-in protection or faster performance. RAID can cause problems, however, and recovering data from a faulty motherboard can be very difficult, so we don't recommend using it here.

AHCI is SATA's native mode and supports advanced features such as Native Command Queuing (NCQ), which intelligently queues all reads and writes to a hard disk to boost performance. This is the best choice if you have SATA hard disks. If AHCI is selected, your hard disks will no longer appear in the Standard CMOS Features menu. Instead, you'll either have a menu called AHCI Configuration (or similar), which will let you view your attached hard disk, or you'll see a different screen when you first turn on your PC that lists your SATA devices.

TIP
If you make a mistake or your settings aren't working, use the Load Fail-Safe Defaults option to reset the BIOS.

```
CMOS Setup Utility - Copyright (C) 1985-2005, American Megatrends, In
                        Boot Sequence

  1st Boot Device        [USB:Crucial]          Help Item
  2nd Boot Device        [HDD:P1-ST31600]
  3rd Boot Device        [USB:SanDisk U3]       Specifies the boot
  4th Boot Device        [CD/DVD:P0-TSST]       sequence from the
  5th Boot Device        [USB:SanDisk U3]       available devices.
  Boot From Other Dev
                         Options                device enclosed in
                   USB:Crucial                  renthesis has been
                   HDD:P1-ST3160023AS           abled in the
                   USB:SanDisk U3 Contour       rresponding type
                   CD/DVD:P0-TSSTcorpCD/DVDW-SH-S1  u
                   USB:SanDisk U3 Contour
                   Disabled



  ↑↓←→:Move  Enter:Select  +/-/:Value  F10:Save  ESC:Exit  F1:General Help
  F4: CPU Spec   F5:Memory-Z   F8:Fail-Safe Defaults   F6:Optimized Default
```

↑ You need to tell your BIOS which device you want to boot from first

A word of warning about AHCI, though: if you already have an operating system installed, changing the SATA mode to AHCI from IDE will cause your computer to crash. If you're planning to install your operating system from scratch, however, AHCI is a good option. The only caveat is that some older motherboards don't support DVD drives when using AHCI, so you may need an IDE optical drive. If you're in any doubt at all, leave the SATA mode as IDE.

SETTING THE BOOT ORDER

To configure how you want your computer to boot, you need to edit the Boot Sequence Order in the Advanced BIOS Features menu. This will be a separate menu option or simply part of the Advanced BIOS Feature menu. Editing these options will let you select which device you want to boot from first. For installing a new operating system and running bootable discs, it makes sense to set the first boot device as your optical drive. Press Enter on 1st Boot Device and make sure that CD/DVD (or similar) is selected.

The second boot device should be your hard disk. Depending on your BIOS, there are two ways to do this. First, you'll either be able to select the physical hard disk from which you want to boot (you may need to take your disk out and look at the model number to make sure you have the right one), or you'll only be able to select Hard Disk. For the latter option, look for a Hard Disk Boot Priority menu. This will let you select the boot order of all the hard disks in your computer. This can be a useful tool: if you're running multiple operating systems installed on different hard disks, for example, you can simply select which one you want to boot from in the BIOS without having to mess around with boot managers or other complex software.

Finally, you can set your BIOS to boot from compatible USB drives. This can be complex, and the procedure depends on your computer. Modern BIOSes will detect USB keys as hard disks, so that you can simply select your USB key as the first device to boot from. Older motherboards don't have such good support, and you may find that your USB key is not supported. You may also find that older USB keys often can't be detected by a BIOS correctly. You'll need to take booting from USB devices on a case-by-case basis.

OTHER DEVICES

The BIOS allows you to configure which other devices on your motherboard are currently in use. The settings for these will be in the Integrated Peripherals menu. Here you'll see options for things such as the HD Audio Controller. You should disable devices that you won't use.

If you've added a dedicated sound card, for example, select HD Audio Controller, Disabled from the menu. You shouldn't need to disable too many devices, but look for outdated devices that you're unlikely to need, such as COM ports (also called serial ports and used to connect to older peripherals, such as PDAs, before USB), and parallel ports (used for old printers).

If you're not using these ports, you can disable them, as they otherwise waste system resources. Simply select a port, such as COM Port 1 (this may be in a separate I/O devices menu) and select Disabled. Repeat for the other ports that you're not using.

If you're using a USB keyboard, look for an option to enable it. If you don't, you'll find that your keyboard won't work after the BIOS has done its Power On Self Test (POST) and before Windows starts, such as when you're running the Windows installer.

READY TO BOOT

With these basic settings configured, you're now ready to boot from your PC. Before you do,

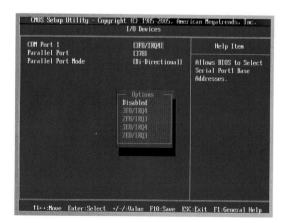

↑ Disable any legacy ports you don't need to use

↑ Keep any changes before you boot your PC

↑ You can check your processor's rated speed in Windows' Control Panel

however, we'll show you how to save your BIOS settings. Go back to the BIOS's main menu and you'll see an option called Save & Exit Setup. Select this and choose OK on the next menu to apply your changes. Your computer will reset and start booting. Alternatively, if you've made a change you didn't want to, you can simply select Exit Without Saving instead.

If the settings you've made have stopped your computer from booting or you're experiencing other problems, you can go back into the menu and select Load Fail-Safe Defaults or Load Optimized Defaults instead. The former selects simple settings that should work with all hardware; the latter option sets slightly more powerful options. In both cases, you'll need to configure your BIOS from scratch.

ADVANCED BIOS CONFIGURATION

Perhaps the most important job that your BIOS does is to tell your PC how fast the processor and memory should run. If these settings are incorrect, you may find that your computer either runs more slowly than it should, or it will run faster but could crash intermittently. It's therefore important to make sure that your BIOS is configured correctly.

PROCESSOR SPEED

To check your processor's speed, you first need to find the correct setting. This may be in a dedicated menu, such as Cell Menu, or listed under Advanced BIOS Features. Whether you're running an Intel or AMD processor, its overall speed is based on two settings: an external bus speed and a multiplier (often called the processor ratio in the BIOS).

The external bus speed multiplied by the multiplier gives you your processor's speed. For

example, a Core 2 Duo E8500 has a clock speed of 3.16GHz. This is made up of an external bus speed of 333MHz multiplied by a x9 multiplier (9 x 333MHz = 3.16GHz).

If either of these settings is incorrect, your computer won't run at its designated speed. In addition, if the external bus speed is incorrect, it will have a knock-on effect on your memory's speed. It's therefore important to make sure that this setting is correct. First, you'll need to know how fast your processor should run. The easiest way to do this is to start Windows. Right-click Computer from the Start menu and select Properties. You should see a screen that lists your processor model name followed by '@ xxxGHz'. This is your processor's rated speed in gigahertz. We'll show you how to check processor speeds for all processors below.

For AMD processors, working out the processor speed is simple, as the external bus speed (which will probably called HyperTransport speed in the BIOS) should be set to 200MHz. You can then set the multiplier. This can be done if you know your processor's rated speed in megahertz (multiply its gigahertz rating by 1,000). If you don't know your processor's rated speed, you can find a list of AMD processors at *http://tinyurl.com/amdprocessors*. Typing the model name into Google will also bring up help. Simply divide your processor's rating in megahertz by 200 to get its multiplier.

For Intel Core i3, Core i5 and Core i7 processors, the external bus (probably called base clock or base frequency) should be set to 133MHz. As with AMD's processors above, all you have to do to find out the multiplier is divide your processor's rated speed in megahertz by 133.

TIP
The temperature monitor can be useful in diagnosing problems with your computer: hot PCs will crash more often than cool ones.

↑ The freely downloadable CPU-Z utility enables you to check your processor's current settings

You can find a list of Intel processor speeds at *http://tinyurl.com/intelprocessors*.

To make things even more confusing, older Intel processors often have their frontside bus (FSB) speed quoted. This is quad-pumped, so is four times faster than the external bus speed. To find out your processor's external bus speed, first find out its FSB speed at *http://tinyurl.com/ intelprocessors*. Divide the listed FSB speed by four to get the external bus speed, and divide your processor's speed in megahertz by the external bus speed to get the multiplier.

In your BIOS, find the options for CPU Ratio (or multiplier) and, depending on your processor, the base frequency, FSB or Hyper-Transport speed. Use the plus and minus keys on your keyboard to adjust these settings.

CHECKING YOUR SETTINGS
Your BIOS may display the processor speed based on the settings you've changed. This can help you check you've configured it properly. If not, don't panic as it can be checked in Windows. To do this, save your settings and reboot your computer.

Install CPU-Z (*www.cpuid.com*) if you don't already have it, and run the application. Click on the CPU tab and at the bottom you'll see your processor's current bus speed and multiplier. The multiplier may be lower than expected as modern processors reduce it when your PC isn't busy in order to save power and reduce heat.

To boost the processor to its maximum speed, download Hot CPU Tester (*www.7byte.com*). Install the software and run it, ignoring any messages

↑ You can use the free CPU-Z application to make a note of your memory's supported speeds

↓ Select the correct CPU Base Frequency to get the right processor speed

about buying the full version. Click Burn-in and Run CPU Burn-in. Select CPU-Z and the multiplier will be at its maximum (it may be sluggish to switch to CPU-Z, but don't worry).

Next, check that the Core Speed is set to your processor's correct rating. If it's not and the bus speed is set correctly, you'll need to go back to your BIOS and adjust the processor's multiplier. If the bus speed is incorrect, you'll need to adjust this. You can now click Stop CPU Burn-in on Hot CPU Tester.

MEMORY SETTINGS
Before we go back to the BIOS, it's best to check your memory's correct speed and settings by going back to CPU-Z and clicking on SPD. This reads the configuration from your memory to get the optimal settings. Look at the Max Bandwidth section and note down the megahertz rating (this may be half the speed you're expecting as memory runs at twice its stated bus speed, so DDR2 800MHz actually has a 400MHz clock speed). Look at the timings table and find the Frequency entry that matches your memory's Max Bandwidth speed. Note down all the information in the table, including CAS# Latency, RAS# to CAS# and so on.

Once you have this information, restart your computer and go into the BIOS and the menu you used to configure your processor. Your memory's speed is defined by the processor's external bus speed multiplied by a multiplier called the memory ratio. Change the memory ratio until your memory is set to the correct speed. For example, on a Core 2 Duo E8500 (333MHz), DDR2 800MHz memory should be set to a memory ratio of 1.2

Configuration and Power Interface (ACPI) mode. Look for an ACPI option and set it to S3, rather than S1. This configures your computer so that in Sleep mode it will only supply power to the memory. This means that your computer will only use a few watts of power; in S1 mode pretty much the entire computer remains on in Sleep mode, which wastes power.

Under this option you'll be able to set the Restore On AC Power Loss feature. This tells your computer what to do after it's lost power – after a power cut, for example. Off will leave your PC off, On will make it turn on when power is restored, and Last State will leave your PC off if it was turned off, but otherwise turn it back on.

(1.2x333=400MHz). Your BIOS should then display the correct full memory speed; in other words, it will show 800MHz for DDR2 800MHz RAM, not the 'true' speed of 400MHz.

Some BIOSes don't have a memory ratio setting, but rather have a menu option that lets you select your memory's full speed, such as 800MHz. Simply select the correct speed from the drop-down list.

Next you'll need to adjust the DRAM Timing Mode. This should be set automatically, but some memory defaults to a slower speed to ensure your PC boots up. The memory timings will be the second set of figures you noted down when you were using CPU-Z.

The headings in the BIOS may not match those taken from CPU-Z, and there may even be more headings displayed. What's important is that the timings in the BIOS are in the same order as in CPU-Z. CAS Latency (CL) will be clearly marked. Starting here, set each row to the value in the corresponding row that you noted down. When your memory is correctly configured, you can save the settings and continue.

POWER SETTINGS

The final job in the BIOS is to make sure that your PC is correctly configured to save power. To do this, find the Power Management Setup (or similar) menu. Here you can change the Advanced

↑ Make sure that you select the correct memory ratio in order to run your RAM at its designated speed

TIP
Memory is often detected incorrectly by the BIOS, so check the settings before continuing.

WAKE UP EVENTS

You can also set your BIOS to define which devices can bring your PC out of Sleep mode. All BIOSes have slightly different options. New computers will have an option to remove control from the BIOS and put it entirely on Windows. This requires managing your devices through the Device Manager in Windows, using the Power Management options.

Most devices don't have these options, and you can only select which devices can and can't wake the computer. These will typically include USB devices, PS/2 Keyboard and PS/2 Mouse, plus PCI or PCI Express devices.

We recommend leaving all these settings enabled. You can still manually control which devices in Windows' Device Manager.

CHAPTER 6

INSTALLING AN OPERATING SYSTEM

IT'S VITAL THAT you install your operating system and drivers correctly in order to make your computer reliable and stable. Whether you've chosen Windows 7 or Linux, here we'll show you how to get everything up and running smoothly. We'll also explain how to configure Windows so that your new PC boots faster.

IN THIS CHAPTER

How to install Windows 7   88

Improve Windows
  Media Center   92

Setting up an SSD   96

How to install
  Ubuntu Linux   100

HOW TO...
Install Windows 7

1 START YOUR COMPUTER
Turn on your PC and put the Windows 7 DVD into its optical drive. If you have a new hard disk, the installation routine will load automatically. If you're using an old hard disk with an operating system already on it, you need to press any key when prompted. If you don't, your old operating system will start and you'll have to reset your PC to start the setup wizard. If the new Windows installer doesn't appear, you'll need to access your PC's BIOS. Check the boot options here to make sure your optical drive is listed first.

2 CHOOSE YOUR LANGUAGE OPTIONS
The first screen that appears will ask you which language you want to use. Select English from the drop-down menu. It should change the next drop-down box, but select English (United Kingdom) as the time and currency format if it doesn't. Your keyboard or input method should be set to United Kingdom automatically when you set the language. If it isn't, select United Kingdom from the third drop-down menu. Click Next to continue.

3 INSTALL WINDOWS 7
On the next screen, click 'What to know before installing Windows' if you want additional information about Windows 7. The 'Repair your computer' link starts the repair console, which can fix problems with a current Windows 7 installation. To install Windows 7, click the 'Install now' button.

4 ACCEPT THE LICENCE TERMS
You'll now be prompted to accept the terms. These are long and wordy, but read through them if you want to know what your licence allows. Tick the 'I accept the license terms' box when you're done. Click Next to continue to the next stage.

5 CHOOSE TYPE OF INSTALLATION
On the next screen, you'll be asked which type of installation you want to perform. Upgrade will upgrade your existing version of Windows. It can also be used to repair a damaged Windows 7 installation. However, this option can be run only from inside Windows. For a fresh installation, select Custom (advanced).

6 SELECT HARD DISK

Your hard disk should automatically be detected by Windows 7. If it isn't, click on the Load Driver button and insert the CD, USB key or floppy disk with the relevant driver. You should need to do this only if you're using RAID or you have a new motherboard that Windows doesn't recognise.

If you're using an old hard disk, it's best to start afresh. Select the partition that contains your old operating system, choose Advanced and click Delete. You can also delete any other partitions this way. You're now ready to continue.

For a new disk, or an old disk where you've wiped the existing partitions, you can just select Unallocated Space and click Next. Windows will automatically create the necessary disk partitions and perform the installation. We recommend that you have at least two partitions: one for Windows, and a smaller one for storing backups, drivers and other files you want to keep permanently.

Select the Unallocated Space and click Advanced and then New. You have to select the size of the partition in megabytes (where 1,024MB

is equal to 1GB). Generally, we'd recommend leaving at least 40GB (40,960MB) for the second partition. Subtract the size of second partition you want from the figure in the box, enter the result and click Apply. Select Disk 0 Unallocated Space, click New and Apply again. You'll get a warning that Windows may create extra partitions, but click OK.

You'll now have two partitions: the one you created, and a 100MB System Reserved partition. Click Disk 0 Unallocated Space, New, and then Apply. You now have all the partitions you need.

7 FORMAT DISKS

To make things easier once you've started Windows, you should format your partitions now. Select Partition 2 (the installation will deal with Partition 1 automatically) and click Format. Click OK in the warning box. You'll get a spinning cursor for a few moments while the disk is formatted. Repeat these steps for the second partition and any others you have that you want to wipe (leave all partitions or disks with important data on them alone). When done, click Partition 2 and then Next.

TIP You can use the back arrow in the installation screens to go back and change a previous setting if you've made a mistake.

8 INSTALL WINDOWS FILES
Windows will automatically copy system files and install the necessary drivers to get your PC working on the first partition you created.

9 SET UP USERNAME AND PASSWORD
After the installation files have finished copying, you'll be prompted to type in a username for yourself (you can create more for other users later) and a name for your computer. Enter this information and click Next. On the next screen, you're asked to enter a password.

The password is optional, but if you want to protect your files and ensure that only authorised users can access your PC, it's vital that you have one. Finally, enter a hint that will remind you of your password in case you forget it, and click Next.

10 ENTER PRODUCT KEY
You will now be prompted to type in your product key, which is inside the box in which your copy of Windows came. Leave the 'Automatically activate Windows when I'm online' and click Next.

11 TURN ON WINDOWS UPDATES
Windows now asks whether you want to turn on Windows Updates automatically. The best option is to select 'Use recommended settings'. Next, set the date and time of your computer.

If you chose your location as UK in the Windows installation routine, the time will be set to GMT by default. Then click Next. If Windows picked up your network adaptor correctly and found that your computer was connected to a network, you'll be asked to choose the type of network – for most people, this will be Home network. Windows will then start for the first time.

12 INSTALL MOTHERBOARD DRIVERS
Although Windows is now working, you still need to install all the relevant drivers to make sure that everything will run smoothly. The trick here is to install any drivers that are for Windows 7; only install Windows Vista drivers if a component isn't working, such as your network adaptor.

Start with your motherboard's drivers. If you downloaded these earlier, insert the USB key or disc to which you saved them. If you couldn't do this, insert the driver disc that came with your motherboard and follow the onscreen instructions. You'll need to download the updated drivers later, and then follow these instructions.

For each driver you downloaded, run the associated file. It's best to start with the chipset driver, but the order afterwards doesn't matter. If Windows displays any warning messages, just click OK. Be careful, as some files you download are just archive files that extract the actual driver files on to your hard disk. If this is the case, go to the folder to which the files were extracted and run the Setup program. You'll probably need to restart your PC after each driver installation.

13 INSTALL GRAPHICS CARD DRIVERS
Windows will install its own graphics drivers for any onboard or dedicated cards you have. These are fine for running Windows, but you won't be able to play games properly. For this, you'll need to install the graphics drivers.

Both ATI and Nvidia provide a single driver package. Simply run the file you downloaded. If you couldn't download the drivers earlier, you should do it now. (Follow Step 14 if you need to install a wireless adaptor to get online and then come back to this step.) Restart your computer after the graphics drivers have been installed. Right-click on the desktop, select Screen Resolution and adjust the resolution to match your monitor's native resolution.

14 INSTALL OTHER PERIPHERALS
You can now install your other peripherals. Install the relevant driver files for each device that's plugged into your motherboard. For USB devices, install the driver file first and, when prompted, connect the device to a USB port. If you're in any doubt, you should read the manual that came with

your peripheral. If you've installed a wireless adaptor, make sure you connect it to your wireless network and follow the provided instructions.

15 RUN WINDOWS UPDATE
Click on the Start menu, type Windows Update and click the entry that appears. Click the Check for Updates button, and Windows will connect to Microsoft's update server and detect which updates you need.

Click on View available updates and look at the list. Some will have been preselected as important updates, but there are also some optional ones, including even newer drivers for your hardware. Select what you'd like to update, then click install.

When they've finished downloading and installing and your PC has restarted, you'll have a working copy of Windows 7 that's up to date.

16 CREATE A SYSTEM REPAIR DISC
Windows 7 has an option to let you create a disc to repair problems with the operating system. It's worth doing this now while you've got a working PC. To do this, click on the Start menu and type repair, and click on Create a System Repair Disc. Put a blank CD or DVD into your optical drive and click Create disc process. This will take a few minutes. When it's done, take the disc out, label it clearly and put it somewhere safe.

TIP
Copying the installation files can take more than an hour, so you'll need to be patient while Windows installs.

Improve Windows Media Center

The default installation of Media Center doesn't let you do much, and you can't play downloaded media such as DivX files very easily. Fortunately, it's simple to tweak – here we show you how

WINDOWS MEDIA CENTER is a brilliant application once you've tweaked it to get rid of all of its minor annoyances and added new features with free software. Here we'll show you how to turn Media Center from a useful bit of kit into the best media player you'll ever own.

To make the most of these instructions, you'll need an official Microsoft Media Center Remote (around £30 including VAT from *www.kikatek.com*). We've found that third-party remote controls don't work very well with some of the third-party software we've recommended.

QUICK FIXES
Once you've installed extra software on your computer, we've found that Media Center can often lose screen priority and let the Start menu reappear. Not only is this annoying, but it can actually cause a crash if you're in the middle of watching a video.

This is easy to fix, however. Go to the Tasks section of the main menu and select Media Only and select Yes when prompted. This will force Media Center to run in full-screen mode,

preventing other applications from taking control. To revert to the standard Media Center mode, select the Media Only option again.

If you're using Media Center just for its media capabilities, you should dispense with some of Windows' more irritating automatic features. First, disable automatic updates, otherwise Window may automatically restart your computer. Open System and select Security (Control Panel and Security in Windows Vista). Click Turn automatic updating on or off. Select Never check for updates and click OK. You should still update your computer at regular intervals, but use Windows Update in the Start menu manually.

Finally, we recommend disabling the indexing service, which periodically scans your hard disk for Windows Search, but isn't used by Media Center. To do this, right-click on Computer in the Start menu and select Manage. Expand the Services and Applications section on the left-hand panel and click Services. Double-click Windows Search and change the Startup type from Automatic to Disabled and click Apply. Click the Stop button and then click OK.

↓ Put Media Center into Media Only mode to make sure it's always the most important application

↑ Turn off automatic updates to prevent Windows from restarting your PC automatically

← **Disable Windows Search to prevent your computer from thrashing the hard disk**

PLAYING ALL MEDIA FILES

With the exception of WMV files, Media Center handles videos incredibly badly, and you'll find that even if you install the necessary codecs to play other types of file you won't be able to fast-forward them. Fortunately, it doesn't have to be this way, and with some free software you'll be able to do everything you'd expect.

First, uninstall any video codecs that you've already installed, such as QuickTime and DivX, as you won't need them. Then downloaded and install ffdshow tryouts (*http://ffdshow-tryout.sourceforge. net*) using the application's default settings. This is a free audio and video decoder that will handle pretty much any video format you'll throw at it.

It still won't let you fast-forward videos, though, so you also need to download the Media Center Control Plugin version 6 (*http://damienbt.free.fr*). Make sure you get the right version for your operating system (32- or 64-bit). This application lets you fast-forward all videos, add bookmarks and resume from the last point at which you stopped watching.

Before you install it, download and install Microsoft Visual C++ 2008 SP1 (*http://tinyurl.com/ C2008SP1*). Then install Media Center Control Plugin. When the installation has finished, select the option to launch the Media Control Configuration. Click on the Remote control & keyboard tab. There's currently no option to stop a video from fast-forwarding, so click Add command. In the first drop-down menu, select Stop Fast Forward/Rewind. The next two options can be used to set a keyboard short cut for the action, but skip this and select Play from the Remote button drop-down menu. Click Commit changes.

To complete the basic configuration, click on the ffdshow configuration tab. Click on Apply minimal configuration and then OK, then on Apply recommended configuration and then OK. Click Commit changes and OK, then restart your computer to apply the changes.

After your PC has restarted, you'll find that you can play any video format in Media Center, and be able to fast-forward and rewind them. Coming back to a video at a later date will pop up an option that asks if you want to resume the video. Press 'i' on the remote control and select More, then Media Control. You can use the menu options to set Bookmarks for programmes you're watching, so that you can jump to your favourite scenes later.

IMPROVE VIDEO PICTURE QUALITY

The picture quality of many downloaded videos isn't very good, but fortunately you can fix this. With a DivX video playing, take Media Center out of Media Only mode, use your mouse to put the application into windowed mode (the middle icon

↓ **You need to configure remote commands in the Media Control window**

when you move the mouse to the top right). In the Notification Area you'll see two new icons: a blue ffdshow audio decoder and a red ffdshow video decoder. Double-click the audio one first.

First, set the correct audio settings. Put a tick in the Mixer box and then click Mixer. Select the Output speakers configuration from the drop-down menu. For most PCs with surround sound this should be 3/0/2 – 5 channels, but for 7.1 speakers select 3/2/2. If you have surround sound, you also need to tick the LFE box to send the subwoofer its own signal. Next, click Dolby decoder and select Apply Dolby Pro Logic II decoding to all stereo sources. This will upsample stereo soundtracks to use all of your speakers. Click OK.

Double-click the video icon. For every setting that we show you how to adjust, make sure that Process whole image is selected. Put a tick in the Deinterlacing box and select Cubic interpolation from the drop-down menu. This will deinterlace TV shows to match your TV's progressive mode. Put a tick in Postprocessing, and a tick in Picture Processing and adjust the sliders until you're happy with the picture's colour, brightness and contrast. Downloaded video can look harsh, so put a tick in the Blur & NR (Blur and Noise Reduction)

box. We find that setting Soften to 40 or less and Gradual denoise to 40 or less helps reduce noise and produce a better image.

You can bring out the detail in a video by ticking the Sharpen box. Select unsharp mask and adjust the Strength bar until you're happy (around 25 should do it). Now to make sure that the picture looks as good as possible, you can force ffdshow to upscale video to match your TV's resolution.

Put a tick in Resize & aspect, select Specify horizontal and vertical size, and type in the size of your display in the box below, such as 1,920x1,080 for 1080p TVs. By default the video will maintain its aspect ratio, so old TV shows will have black bars down the side of the picture. If you don't like this, select No aspect ratio correction, to fill the screen. Click Apply. You can now maximise Media Center and use it as normal.

There are a couple of problems with Media Control. First, it will also work when you try to play a DVD, prompting you to launch ffdshow. The idea is that ffdshow can take over the picture processing, increasing quality. However, we've yet to get this to work successfully and have found that it stops DVD menus from working. Just wait for the option to disappear.

↑ The application ffdshow can turn stereo sound into surround sound

↑ You can also improve the quality of your video with ffdshow

Second, when you stop watching a video, pressing fast-forward later on – when you're watching a DVD, for example – will cause your old video to start playing again. To get round this, when you've stopped watching a video, select Media Control from Media Center's main menu and select Restart Media Center. You'll have to put Media Center back into Media Only mode.

TV EVERYWHERE

Media Center can also be used to catch up with TV shows that you may have missed with the free TunerFree MCE application (*www.milliesoft.co.uk/tunerfree.php*). This provides a single interface for all the major catch-up services, including the BBC's iPlayer and Channel 4's 4oD. Download the application for your operating system (Vista or Windows 7), quit Media Center and install TunerFree using the Typical settings. The process will take several minutes as the database of available programmes is downloaded.

Before you can use the software you need to make sure that your computer has all the necessary codecs to play the files. Visit each service at the website below using Internet Explorer and play a sample video, downloading extra software when prompted:

SERVICE	ADDRESS
BBC	www.bbc.co.uk/iplayer
ITV	www.itv.com/ITVPlayer
Channel 4 On Demand	http://www.channel4.com/4od
Five	http://demand.five.tv

When done, you can start Media Center. TunerFree MCE is installed into the TV + Movies section of the main menu. When you launch the application, you can either browse through the individual channels, or use the options at the top to browse by date or search by keyword.

The default installation also lets you select Hulu, which is a US-only service. To fix this, choose Preferences and select Get Hulu so that it has a grey box next to it. Click Save, and then Back. You'll now have access to every TV-on-demand service in the UK.

↑ TunerFree MCE lets you watch all of the UK's TV-on-demand services via Media Center

TIP
Check for TunerFree MCE updates regularly, as new TV services are added all the time.

SOUND IMPROVEMENTS

The final adjustment is improving the sound when watching DVDs. Media Center's built-in audio decoder will let you listen to Dolby Digital soundtracks only if you're using analogue outputs, not DTS. This can be fixed easily, however. Download and install AC3Filter (*http://ac3filter.net*). From the Start menu, run AC3Filter Config. Change the output to match your speaker configuration (surround-sound users should select 3/2+SW 5.1 channels).

The other settings, such as the Equalizer and Mixer for adjusting speaker volume, bass and treble, are best adjusted when you're listening to some audio. AC3Filter puts an icon in the Notification Area when compatible audio is playing, which you can double-click to adjust settings on the fly.

To get AC3Filter working in Media Center requires a bit of fiddling. First, you need to find out the CLSID of the software. You can do this by downloading the DirectShow Filter Manager (*www.softella.com/dsfm/index.en.htm*). Run the software and double-click the entry for AC3Filter. Copy the CLSID including the curly brackets.

Run RegEdit and navigate to HKey_Local_Machine\Software\Microsoft\Windows\CurrentVersion\Media Center\Decoder. Double-click PreferredMPEG2AudioDecoderCLSID and paste in the CLSID you copied earlier. Click OK and shut down RegEdit. Now when you watch a DVD, you'll be able to decode DTS soundtracks.

Setting up an SSD

A solid-state disk can make your computer boot much faster than a traditional hard disk, but it needs configuring in Windows first. Here we show you what to do

A SOLID-STATE DISK (SSD) has a lot of advantages over a traditional mechanical hard disk. SSDs use fast memory chips, so your computer will boot more quickly and Windows and your other applications will load a lot faster. In our tests, we've seen the boot time of Windows 7 fall from 54 to 24 seconds on a Core i5-750 PC simply by switching from a hard disk to an SSD.

Furthermore, SSDs have no moving parts, so they're immune to a lot of the problems from which mechanical disks suffer, such as being damaged by being knocked.

However, SSDs do have a write limit, so you'll need to configure Windows to get the most out of them. Over the next few pages we'll take you through all the settings you need to adjust.

There are some other downsides to using SSDs. You have to pay a lot more per megabyte when buying an SSD, and the largest models are still a lot smaller than regular hard disks. For this reason, it's worth having an SSD for booting and running applications, and a traditional hard disk for storing all your data. We recommend a minimum

BOOT TIMES TESTED

Boot times measured on a Windows 7 PC with a Core i5-750 processor

capacity of 64GB for an SSD, although 128GB is preferable. If you're planning on using an SSD on its own as a single drive, 128GB should be the absolute minimum.

Another problem with SSDs involves the technology they use. Most consumer SSDs use multi-level cell (MLC) memory chips. A cell is an area for storage that's split into pages (typically around 4KB each) and grouped into blocks (usually 128 pages for a total of 512KB). Because of the technology used, each page can be written to individually, but only if it's empty. If a page is considered to have data in it, it has to

➜ For an SSD you need to have AHCI enabled in the BIOS

↑ Move the paging file for virtual memory to a regular hard disk

↑ Move the system index to a regular hard disk if you have one

be erased first. However, only entire blocks can be erased at once.

This causes an issue whereby overwriting a file means the original data has to be wiped first. So, an SSD has to read the existing block, wipe the storage space and write back the data. This can cause problems with performance, as there's more of an overhead involved in writing data. It can also cause longevity problems; MLC cells have a lifespan of only around 10,000 writes. After this, a cell can't be written to or erased, although the data can be read, so an SSD that has been worn out completely can still be read. To erase data securely, the disk has to be physically destroyed. Information about cells wearing out has led to a lot of panic about the quality and usability of SSDs, but it's mostly unfounded.

According to research, MLC drives last a lot longer than you might think. According to a test performed by Toshiba, a typical user will write up to 2.4GB per day and a heavy user will write up to 9.2GB per day, including autosave and hibernate features in the operating system. Taking this into account, SSDs are rated to last at least three years, for up to 20GB of data per day; for a typical

user writing 2.4GB per day, that's a life span of 25 years, which should be plenty.

This longevity is achieved in several ways. First, if you're using an operating system that supports it, such as Windows 7, there's the TRIM command. This allows the operating system to tell the SSD which blocks are considered free in the file system, enabling the disk's controller to take care of overwrites. Second, wear levelling ensures that data is spread evenly over a disk so that one cell doesn't wear out before the others.

However, you will need to perform some extra configuration to make your SSD last as long as possible; this includes disabling systems that constantly write to a disk, such as virtual memory – we'll show you how using Windows 7. We've split the guide into two parts: one for systems that have more than one disk (an SSD and a hard disk) and one for systems with just an SSD.

INSTALLING WINDOWS

An SSD will be smaller than your existing hard disk, so you must decide how to transfer your operating system. Most SSDs come as a kit with cloning software that will do the job for you, but this requires that the amount of data on your hard disk is equal to or less than the capacity of the SSD. If it isn't, you'll need to move some files off the hard disk until there's enough room. For this reason, the best option is a fresh installation of Windows 7.

Before you install Windows 7, make sure that the advanced host controller interface (AHCI) is turned on in the BIOS (see page 78). This is the SATA native mode and supports all the advanced features that SSDs require. It's usually found in the menu with storage options. Make sure that your BIOS is set so the SSD is the primary boot hard disk after the optical drive.

Windows should detect your SSD and disable defragmentation (which can damage it), but you should check. Open Computer, right-click your SSD and select Properties, then click Tools. Click Defragment now, click Configure schedule, then click Select disks. Make sure that your SSD is

↑ Windows 7 makes it easy to move your user files to another hard disk

deselected; Windows should automatically remove your SSD from this list, so don't worry if you can't see it.

USING AN SSD WITH A TRADITIONAL DISK
The chances are you'll be adding an SSD to a computer with a hard disk. This gives you both speed and lots of storage. Once you've got Windows up and working, you can work through making the system changes. First, make sure virtual memory is turned off on the SSD. Virtual memory saves data from RAM to the hard disk to free up space for other applications, but it can hammer a disk. Right-click Computer in the Start menu and select Properties. Click the System protection link, select Advance and then click Setting under Performance. Click the Advanced tab and click Change. Untick the 'Automatically manage paging file size for all drives' option. Click C:, select 'No paging file' and then click Set. You should see a warning telling you that your computer could run out of memory, but click OK. Repeat for any partitions on your SSD.

Now you need to turn on virtual memory for a hard disk. Select an internal hard disk, such as D: and click System managed size, then click Set. Click OK on all the open dialog boxes.

Next you need to sort out Indexing. This is the service that indexes all your files so you can find them quickly and can be responsible for quite a few file writes. Click on the Start menu and type Index. Click on Advanced, Indexing options and 'Select new' under 'Index location'. Browse to a regular hard disk and click OK. The index can only be moved to the root of a drive and the changes won't stick if you select a folder.

It's worth moving your Documents, Pictures, Music and Videos folders to a hard disk to save space on your SSD. Windows 7 makes this easy using Libraries. To move the Documents folder, go to your physical hard disk and make a folder for files, such as d:\documents or d:\<yourname>\ documents. To change the location of your Documents folder, type Libraries into the Start menu and click Libraries. Right-click Documents and select Properties. Click Include a folder, navigate to your new folder and click Include

↑ Disable virtual memory on a laptop to prolong the life of the SSD

↑ You can disable Windows Search, but we don't recommend it

folder. Select the existing entries in the 'Library locations' window, select Remove and click OK.

Use the above instructions for the Music, Pictures, and Videos Libraries. Once done, every time you access one of these Libraries you'll be diverted to the new folder on your mechanical hard disk. There's little point in changing other user settings or hunting for a way to move the Windows Temp folder and Program files. You may want to consider moving the default download directory of your web browser, though, so it saves files to your hard disk rather than the SSD.

USING AN SSD ON ITS OWN

If you've decided to build your computer with only an SSD, your configuration options are more limited, as you can't move files to another disk. This means you have to disable some services. It's worth disabling virtual memory, as this can harm an SSD. To do this, you'll need 4GB of RAM, or Windows could run out of memory. You can

TIP
You should never defragment an SSD, as this can cause permanent damage.

leave it enabled if you have less RAM, but you could wear out your SSD more quickly.

Right-click Computer in the Start menu and select Properties. Click System protection, select Advanced and click Setting under Performance. Click the Advanced tab and then click Change. Untick the 'Automatically manage paging file size for all drives' option. You'll be prompted to restart. In Windows, follow the instructions above to get back to the Virtual Memory dialog box and click C:, select 'No paging file' and click Set.

You can't move the Indexing service on a laptop, but you can disable it. However, we don't recommend it, as it will be hard to find programs and files. If this doesn't bother you and you want to disable the service, click on the Start menu and type in Services. Click Services from the list and double-click Windows Search in the list. Select Disabled from the Startup type drop-down box, then click the Stop button and OK to continue. It's not worth making any other changes.

HOW TO...
Install Ubuntu Linux

1 DOWNLOAD UBUNTU

Linux is regularly updated, so check the website *www.ubuntu.com/getubuntu* to download the latest version. Make sure you pick the right version for your computer (32-bit or 64-bit). Essentially, unless your processor supports only 32-bit operating systems, you should download the 64-bit OS.

Once you've downloaded the correct ISO (disc image) files, you'll need to burn it to a CD before you can use it. We recommend using CDBurnerXP, which is a free download from *http://cdburnerxp. se*. Alternatively, you can use the free UNetbootin utility (*http://unetbootin.sourceforge.net*) to create a bootable USB flash drive with the ISO image.

You don't need to commit to using Linux at this stage; if you just want to give it a try, you can run it directly from your installation disc (see Step 3 for more details).

2 BOOT FROM THE CD

Put the Ubuntu CD that you've created into your optical drive and wait for the 'Press any key to boot from CD' message. If you miss this message, you'll have to restart your computer to load the Ubuntu installation routine. The first splash screen should load very quickly. If you don't get this message, you'll need to go into your PC's BIOS and change the boot options to make the CD the first boot device (see page 78).

3 START THE INSTALLATION

You'll now be presented with a Language menu and a choice of two options. The default installation option is to try Ubuntu without making any changes to your computer. This simply loads Ubuntu from the CD and doesn't write any files to your hard disk.

This is an excellent way to try out Linux before commiting yourself fully to operating system and filling up your hard disk, and is the wisest option if you're not totally sure about whether Linux is for you. You can't do too much to the OS, but it's a good way to get a feel for it before you commit to it. If you do want to install Ubuntu properly, select the Install Ubuntu option.

4 CHECK INSTALLATION CRITERIA

You'll now see a splash screen that has a list of criteria to make the installation go as smoothly as possible. Make sure your computer is connected to the internet, as this allows it to download the latest updates. Select Download updates while installing to force this option, and you'll save yourself time in the long run.

For the best results, Ubuntu will need to install some third-party software in order to be able to play MP3, Flash and other multimedia files. Select Install this third-party software and click Forward.

5 ERASE HARD DISK
If your hard disk has any other operating system installed on it, you'll see a warning on the next screen. You'll have the option to install Ubuntu alongside your existing OS or, if you're running Ubuntu already, upgrade it.

For the best results, select the Erase option. This will wipe your hard disk and let you start from scratch. This saves any confusion in the future of having more than one operating system on the hard disk. Be warned, however, that erasing your hard disk will mean you'll lose all data currently on it, so make sure you have a backup of your important files before you select this option. When you're ready, click Forward.

6 CHOOSE PARTITION SIZES
Ubuntu uses a simple partitioning system on your PC's hard disk. Tweaking this will enable you to choose where your user files are kept and to create separate partitions for program files and virtual memory. Linux stores user files in the /home folder, and moving this to its own partition is easy. However, if you opt to set up one partition manually, you'll have to set them all up this way.

If you want to stick with Ubuntu's default option, click Install Now and skip to Step 12.

7 MANUALLY ERASE PARTITIONS
To define your hard disk's partitions manually, select the advanced partitioning tool. The installer will scan your hard disk and display the disk partitioning tool. The first step is to delete all the existing partitions on the hard disk, so select each one in the list and click the Delete button. If you have more than one hard disk in your PC, your first disk is /dev/sda or dev/hda (dev/sdb or dev/hdb is your second disk). You should configure the first disk in your system, generally. If your disks are in the wrong order, you can switch the internal SATA cables to fix this.

TIP You can try Ubuntu without installing it. Simply boot off the CD and explore the desktop. When you're ready to proceed, you just need to run the installer.

8 CREATE BOOT PARTITION

You should now have free space listed under /dev/sda. Since we're making partitions by hand, we need to create all the partitions that Linux requires, starting with the /boot partition. Select free space in the list of partitions and click New. Enter a size of 50 (we're working in megabytes) and then select /boot as the mount point. Click OK to continue.

9 CREATE SWAP PARTITION

Linux also needs a /swap partition, which is the equivalent of the Windows swap file used for virtual memory. When your PC's real memory fills up, Ubuntu will swap bits of the memory that aren't currently being used – such as RAM being used for inactive applications, for example – to the hard disk. This gives the impression that your computer has more memory than it actually does, enabling you to run more applications.

First, create another new partition in the free space and then enter a size (in megabytes) that is equal to the amount of RAM in the computer, remembering that one gigabyte is 1,024MB. Select Swap area from the 'Use as' drop-down list, leave the other settings at their defaults and click OK.

10 CREATE HOME PARTITION

Next, you need to set the /home partition, which is where user files are kept. This is the equivalent of Windows' My Documents folder, but it is kept on a separate partition. The advantage of this method is that if you ever need to reinstall Linux, you can do so and your documents won't be overwritten.

Make this partition as large as you like, but make sure you keep around 15GB free for the final /root partition. Select /home as the mount point before clicking OK.

11 SET ROOT PARTITION

The final custom partitioning task you need to perform is to set the root or / partition. This is where Ubuntu is installed, and it will use all the remaining space. Set the mount point as / and click OK. You can see the final partition structure from the screen above. Click Install Now when you're ready to continue.

12 SET CONFIGURATION SETTINGS

Ubuntu will now start installing to your computer. While it's copying files, you need to specify a few settings. First, you need to set your current location on a map of the world in order for

Ubuntu to set the date and time correctly. You can also start typing the name of your town or city into the text box. Click Forward when you've done this. Next you'll be asked to configure your keyboard and mouse settings by selecting the language and type from the list. Click Forward when you're done.

13 SET USERNAME AND PASSWORD

You'll now be prompted to enter a username and password for your computer. Enter your password twice, and Ubuntu will tell you if it's a weak, fair or strong password. You can now change the name of your PC.

You then need to decide how you want to log in. Logging in automatically will boot straight to the desktop, but the 'Require my password to log in' option is much more secure. If you choose the latter option, you can also select 'Encrypt my home folder' for extra security. However, if you forget your user password, your files will be completely locked and you'll be unable to recover them. Only choose this option if security is a paramount concern. Click Forward when you're ready.

14 FINALISE INSTALL

With your configuration options set, Ubuntu will now go through the process of finalising the installation and copying the remaining files to your hard disk. This process takes a fair while, so you can leave it copying.

15 MANAGE SOFTWARE

Once Ubuntu has finished installing, go to the Software Centre, the online app store available from the Launcher on the left-hand side of the screen, to find and install new programs. New applications are downloaded from the internet using an intuitive package manager. Any additional components (known as dependencies) are automatically downloaded and installed. Applications already installed can also be removed using this tool.

16 INSTALL UPDATES

Because of its rising popularity, Ubuntu Linux is attracting some interest from malicious hackers, so you need to make sure the latest security patches are installed.

Ubuntu has its own update manager and checks periodically for updates. When new updates become available, you'll see a warning on the application bar. Click on the warning to bring up the list of updates and then click the Install Updates button.

TIP

Finding drivers for all your hardware can be difficult, but a Google search should bring up some forums that may be able to help you get your hardware working.

WINDOWS 7 IS Microsoft's latest operating system and one of the best choices for a new PC. While it's similar in many ways to previous versions of Windows, it adds many new features. Here we'll show you what some of these new features are and how you can use them.

IN THIS CHAPTER

The desktop   106

Manage your windows   107

How to transfer your files   108

Keeping track of files   110

Sharing files with
    HomeGroup   112

How to perform an
    Anytime Upgrade   114

The desktop

Gadgets

Gadgets display simple bits of information, such as the current weather and the time. You can add more by right-clicking the desktop and selecting Gadgets.

Preview windows

Hovering the mouse cursor over a highlighted icon displays a preview of the application's current windows. Hovering the cursor over one of these previews brings that window to the foreground for a better view.

Start menu

Windows 7's Start menu is similar to Vista's. You use it to find programs, documents and Control Panel items. The Shut down button is there to turn off your computer, but you can click the arrow next to it to switch users, hibernate your PC and more besides.

Running taskbar icon

Highlighted icons show you which applications are currently running.

Taskbar icons

Non-highlighted icons in the taskbar are used to launch commonly used applications. You can drag and drop your favourite programs here from the Start menu.

Jump Lists

If you right-click on a taskbar icon you'll see a Jump List, which gives you quick access to recently accessed documents, folders, websites, songs, pictures and more.

Manage your windows

Grab an application and shake the mouse to minimise all other open windows. This is a great way to clear clutter onscreen, so you can focus on a single application. Do the same thing again to restore the other windows.

Grab an application and move it to either side so it takes up half your monitor. This is a quick way to compare two applications side by side. Move a window to the top of the screen and it's maximised to take up the whole screen. You can select a window and press Windows and → ← or ↑ for the same effect.

Move your mouse cursor to the bottom right of the screen and all the windows dissolve to an outline. Use this mode to view gadgets quickly and see how many windows you have open. Click the left mouse button to minimise all windows, and click it again to bring them back.

HOW TO...
Transfer your files

Copying files and settings from your old system to your new PC is a breeze thanks to Windows 7's Easy Transfer wizard

YOU MAY BE building a brand new PC using the very latest components, but chances are that you have an old computer that's set up just the way you like it. However, with Windows 7 on your new computer you don't have to start completely from scratch. You can copy over your documents, media files, web bookmarks and so on using Windows 7's Easy Transfer wizard. This helps you copy files and settings from your old system to the new one, regardless of whether or not they're on the same machine.

1 RUN EASY TRANSFER
If you're running Vista on your old PC, you already have Easy Transfer. Launch it from the Start menu via All Programs, Accessories, System Tools. In XP, you'll need to insert your Windows 7 disc. Close the installer if it opens, then go to My Computer, right-click on the DVD drive and select Explore (not Open). Browse to the Support folder, then the Migwiz folder. Double-click on the file called migsetup.exe and the Easy Transfer Wizard will start. A welcome screen helpfully explains all the merits of Windows Easy Transfer; feel free to read it, then click Next.

You'll need some form of external storage to house your files during the transfer. If you plan to copy only a small quantity of data, you may be able to use a CD, a DVD or a USB flash drive, but you probably have too many files. In this case, the easiest option is an external USB hard disk, although if your computer is on a network you can use another PC or a network-attached storage (NAS) device. Choose the appropriate method from the choices given. In Vista, confirm that this is your old computer, rather than the new system.

The wizard now scans your system to see what files and settings can be transferred and shows the results in a list. In our example it's divided files into My items (those belonging to our user account) and Shared items. Click Customize to see a list of all the kinds of files that will be backed up, such as desktop items, favourites and program settings. If you don't want a particular item kept, deselect it. For finer control, click Advanced at the bottom.

2 SAVE YOUR DATA
Having chosen the files to keep, click through and you'll be asked if you want to protect your backup with a password. Unless there are sensitive

➔ Easy Transfer helps you move your documents, settings, emails and more from your old PC

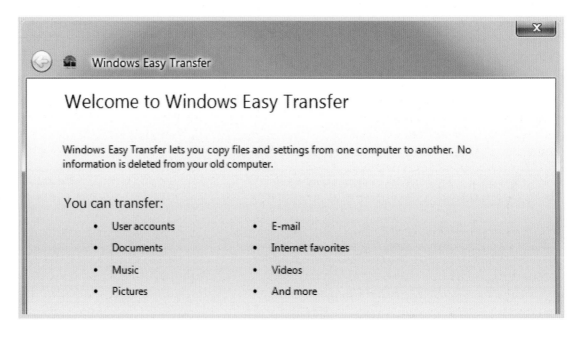

Windows Easy Transfer

Welcome to Windows Easy Transfer

Windows Easy Transfer lets you copy files and settings from one computer to another. No information is deleted from your old computer.

You can transfer:

- User accounts
- Documents
- Music
- Pictures

- E-mail
- Internet favorites
- Videos
- And more

files, skip this. You'll be asked to name your set of data; choose something you'll recognise later, such as 'Windows XP transfer', and browse to where you'll save your data, as discussed in step 2. In our case it's a USB stick.

You can now start the transfer. A window shows you the progress, which may take some time. You're then told if any files didn't copy; if you need them, copy them manually to a USB drive or other storage for future use.

If you haven't yet installed Windows 7 on your new PC, follow the steps on pages 88 to 91, and come back when you're ready to retrieve your data.

3 RUN EASY TRANSFER IN WINDOWS 7
On your new system, click the Start orb and go to All Programs, Accessories, System Tools. Click on Windows Easy Transfer, click through the welcome window and you'll be asked what method you're using. Select the storage you used, and say

TIP
Your programs won't be included in the transfer process unless you install Windows 7 over a matching edition of Vista and pick the Upgrade option. Otherwise you'll have to reinstall each application from its original disc or download, or use a utility such as LapLink PCmover (*www. laplink.com/pcmover*). This is because program installations involve system files.

this is your new PC. When asked if your files have already been saved to an external drive, plug in your media and click Yes. (If you backed up over a network, make the appropriate choice.)

Select the storage type, browse to your storage device and navigate to the folder you selected earlier. You should see the file you named in step 2 ('Windows XP transfer', or whatever) with the label 'Easy Transfer File'. Select this and enter your password, if you chose one.

4 RESTORE YOUR DATA
Windows 7 scans your backup and shows a window as in step 1. Choose what to restore, or leave everything selected. Click Advanced for tasks such as transferring a whole user account from the old system or mapping an entire drive from Windows XP. Click Transfer to begin the final stage. At the end you'll see confirmation of exactly what was transferred.

Keeping track of files

Windows 7's Libraries organise all your documents for you, helping you to keep your new computer neat and tidy

THOUGH YOU MAY never have known you needed them, Libraries are one of the best things about Windows 7. There are four categories by default: Documents, Music, Pictures and Video. Each section contains all the folders and files you would previously have kept in the relevant folder in My Documents (in Windows XP) or Documents (in Windows Vista).

What's different is that the items in a Library don't have to be stored in the same place. They don't even have to be on your PC's main hard disk. You can include files and folders from anywhere – perhaps an external drive, or another computer on your network – in the same Library.

To see this in action, expand the Documents subfolder within Libraries by clicking the blue disclosure triangle that appears beside Documents when you hover over it. You'll see two entries: My Documents and Public Documents. (These are actual disk folders; right-click on My Documents and you'll see it lives in C:\Users\Name, where Name is your Windows username.)

By default, each Library location includes two folders: My Documents and Public Documents, My Video and Public Video and so on. If you click the 'Library locations' link, you can add a folder and bring its contents into the Library from anywhere. This doesn't move the folder itself, yet the items appear in your Library as if they were all in one place. If you rename or delete something in the Library view, this has the expected effect on the actual item, wherever it's stored.

It's by adding your own items to Libraries that they become truly useful, pulling together items from across your system in categories that make sense to you. The only limitation is the inability to add folders on removable storage, such as a USB flash drive or a DVD. However, you can include folders on other PCs on your network or on a network-attached storage (NAS) box.

Just ike the Documents or My Documents folders in previous versions of Windows, Libraries belong to an individual user account. As soon as you have more than one user on your computer, however, you should really have more than one user account. This means everyone will be able to

have their own files in their own places, which others – except an Administrator – won't be able to mess with. This makes extra sense with Windows 7's Libraries. Each family member can arrange their own things as they like, and even put shared files that everybody uses, such as the family music collection, into their own Libraries, organised their own way.

Assuming you're the Administrator, everyone else should have a Standard account, which they should log in with every time they use the PC (to switch accounts, click the Start orb, click the triangle next to Shut down and choose Switch user). Standard users can't install software or change system settings – they'll have to ask you to enter your Administrator password. They can set their own desktop background, for example, use software already on the PC, save their own web bookmarks and edit and delete their own files.

You can also set up a Guest account, with similarly limited privileges, for anyone who needs to use the PC on an ad hoc basis.

1 CREATE A USER ACCOUNT
Hit the Windows key and type 'user accounts', then click on User Accounts when it appears. Select Manage Another Account, Create New Account. Type the name of the person and make sure Standard user is selected, then click Create Account.

All accounts should be protected by a password, so people can't log in as each other. If a user forgets their password, the Administrator can reset it. Go back to Manage Another Account, click the name of your new user and choose Create A Password. You'll also be asked for a hint that the user will see if they forget the correct password. Change the picture, too, if you like.

2 SETP UP CONTROLS
You can also apply Parental Controls from here. For example, you can set a maximum age rating for games, so a user won't be allowed to run unsuitable titles, even if they're already installed on the PC. (This setting uses the BBFC and PEGI ratings applied to all games sold

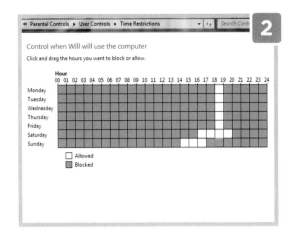

commercially in the UK.) You can also specify which individual games or applications users can access. You can even dictate the exact times of the day and week at which they will and won't be allowed to use the computer.

When the user runs up against one of the controls you've put in place, they'll be invited to contact you if they want to ask you to override it. Of course, it's up to you whether to do so.

If you need more comprehensive controls, Windows Live Family Safety adds web filtering and activity reporting. This is available as part of Microsoft's free Live add-ons.

3 ADD FOLDERS

By default, the only folders in each Library are the standard Documents locations under C:\ Users\. To add folders, click the 'Includes 2 locations' link at the top of a Library view. Then Click Add to start expanding the Library. You can add folders from almost any location, including network folders. The only ones you can't add are removable storage devices such as USB memory drives and optical drives (CDs and DVDs).

TIP
Parental Controls take the user accounts concept to its logical conclusion by enabling you to decide exactly what each user can and can't do on the computer. Of course, this is no substitute for human supervision; Windows is clever, but it lacks your parental judgement. Insofar as you do rely on user account controls, remember that if a user knows your Administrator name and password they can simply log in as you, so make sure you keep these details secret.

4 SAVE LOCATIONS

As we've already mentioned, the strength of Libraries is that they bring together content that's stored in different places. But what if you actually want to store something in the Library? You can: drag a folder on to your Documents Library, for example, and it moves there. You can have lots of physical files and folders within a Library as well as other locations. They all get stored in the default save location. In the Documents Library Locations dialog box, one of the folders will be marked as the default save location. That's the physical folder to which any files dragged into the Library will be saved. To change it, all you need to do is right-click on another Library folder and select Set as default save location.

Note that if you right-click on an already created Library and select New Folder, that's what you get: a new folder in the default save location.

You're not limited to the supplied Libraries. To make a new Library, click on the top-level Libraries icon, right-click and select New, Library. Enter a name. Your Library won't include any folders until you add some.

Sharing files with HomeGroup

Sharing files and resources between several computers is simple with the help of Windows 7's HomeGroup feature

EXPERIENCED WINDOWS USERS will know that file and printer sharing is a well-established technology, though it's only really become commonplace in the home and small office in the past few years, as multiple PCs have become the norm. However, setting up file sharing has always been a tricky business, requiring you to tackle user accounts, permissions and workgroups. Windows 7 makes it much easier with a new system called HomeGroup.

Simply put, a homegroup is a collection of computers that can access the files in one another's Libraries. The beauty of HomeGroup is that, unlike with the previous Windows file-sharing system, at no point do you need to know the name or network address of any of the computers with which you want to share files.

Once your homegroup is up and running, you'll see it in the Windows Explorer navigation pane, with a list of all the other computers in your homegroup that are online. Simply click on one and you'll be able to access its Libraries as if they were your own. You can even incorporate files from your homegroup into your own Library.

↓ HomeGroups make it easy to share files and printers between Windows 7 PCs

This could raise some concerns about the security of your files, so there are a few points we should make clear. First, you don't have to share all your Libraries: on each PC, you can choose which of your Pictures, Videos, Music or Documents Libraries to share. By default, Documents is disabled, so you can let other family members listen to your Dire Straits albums without giving them the ability to snoop on your bank statements. You can also manually mark specific files or folders as private to prevent access.

As an extra level of security, all the folders you share will be read-only to other users in the group, so you don't need to worry about anyone accidentally deleting or corrupting your files. Nor will the kids be able to fill your hard disk with temporary files and unwanted downloads. If you do want to enable other users to edit a particular file, or let them add files to one of your folders, that's easy to set up.

The bane of any file-sharing arrangement has always been that the PC containing the files you want might be switched off. Even Windows 7, clever though it is, hasn't cracked the challenge of talking to a system that's powered down. The good news, however, is that there's a workaround: while browsing files or folders that reside on a different PC, you can tell Windows to make them available offline. After you do this, you'll find that, magically, you can access them even when the other computer isn't available.

Of course, there's a trick to it. When you make a file from another machine available offline, Windows creates a hidden copy of it on your own hard disk. Later, if it can't access the file over the network, it silently shows you this local copy instead. It all happens transparently. The other user might change the file, of course, but Windows synchronises its copy with the original whenever it can – and files won't get changed on the other PC while it's turned off. So for most purposes it's just like working with the actual file.

HomeGroup beats Windows Vista's file-sharing wizards because it requires very little configuration. The catch is that it works only with other Windows 7 PCs, but if that's what you have it'll save you a huge amount of effort. Standard file sharing can still be used with other machines.

1 MAKE YOURSELF AT HOME
Windows 7 should prompt you to create a homegroup the first time each PC connects to a network. You can only use HomeGroup if you're on a network designated as Home, rather than Work or Public. You can set this option in the Network and Sharing Center under 'View your active networks'.

2 CREATE A HOMEGROUP
Now go to Control Panel and select Network and Internet, then HomeGroup. Click Create HomeGroup. Select 'Libraries to share' and click

TIP HomeGroup is designed to be as easy to use as possible. However, this means it's not very versatile. When you share files and folders, your sharing settings affect everybody in the group. If you want to create a more complex sharing system – for example, to give your partner access to your Documents Library but not your children – you have to go back to the old way of sharing folders.

Next. Save the default password or make up your own secure password.

3 ADD PCs
On another Windows 7 PC, bring up HomeGroup from the Control Panel. Click Join HomeGroup. Select 'Libraries you want to share from this PC' and click Next. Type the password you provided in step 2 and click Next. Once the PC is connected to the homegroup, you can share files and printers with your other machines via the HomeGroup icon in Windows Explorer.

4 CHOOSE WHAT TO SHARE
To alter which files are available for sharing, open HomeGroup from the Control Panel. You can also choose to make your media available to network-streaming devices. To stop sharing a file or folder, click on the 'How do I exclude files and folders?' link for instructions.

HOW TO...
Perform an Anytime Upgrade

There's no reason to be stuck with the same version of Windows 7 forever. With the help of Microsoft's Anytime Upgrade feature, you can take advantage of the benefits of other versions as your needs change

WHEN YOU INSTALL Windows 7, you install all the features of every version – it's just that some features are locked. However, with Anytime Upgrade you can upgrade your version of Windows 7 instantly simply by buying a new licence key. The Home Premium edition can be upgraded to Professional or Ultimate, while Professional can be upgraded to Ultimate.

The beauty of this type of upgrade is that you don't need to reinstall any software, and your files are left intact on your computer along with your Windows settings. For a full breakdown of the prices, go to *http://emea.microsoftstore.com/uk*.

1 RUN UPGRADE APPLICATION
Click on the Start menu and type Upgrade. Then select Windows Anytime Upgrade from the search results. Selecting 'Go online to choose the edition of Windows 7 that's best for you' lets you buy a new product upgrade key online and upgrades your computer. Meanwhile, selecting 'Enter an upgrade key' lets you type in an upgrade product key, such as the one provided in a retail Windows Anytime Upgrade box; we'll assume this is the choice you've made.

2 ENTER THE UPGRADE KEY
On the next screen, type in the Upgrade key you were given and click Next. Once the key has been verified, you'll be prompted to accept the licence terms. Click 'I accept'. You'll then see a warning telling you that the process takes about 15 minutes and advising you to close all open applications and save your work. Once you've done this, click Upgrade.

3 INSTALL NEW FEATURES
Your PC checks online to see if any updates are available before upgrading your version of Windows 7. It then begins the main upgrade procedure, which will take a few minutes. Once it's complete, your PC will restart and Windows will reload with the features of the new version unlocked. You'll see a welcome screen with a link to help you find out about the new features.

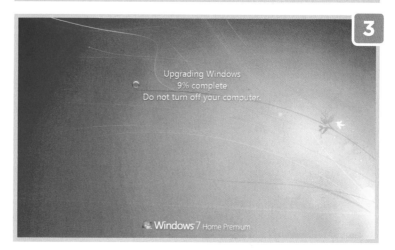

TRY COMPUTER SHOPPER
WITH 3 ISSUES FOR £1

Right now you can claim the next 3 issues for just £1! It's a 100% risk free offer because if after 3 issues you're not completely satisfied you can write to cancel your subscription and you **won't pay any more than the £1 already debited**.

YOUR GREAT DEAL

- **3 issues for £1** to start your subscription
- If you're not satisfied, simply cancel and **pay no more than the £1** already debited
- **Save up to 26%** on the shop price if you continue
- **FREE delivery** to your door
- Get every issue **before it hits the shops**

ORDER ONLINE TODAY AT:
www.dennismags.co.uk/computershopper

OR CALL NOW ON
0844 844 0031

Quoting offer code
G1110BUI

SO YOUR NEW PC is up and running and you've installed your operating system, but you're not quite finished if you want the best setup possible. In this chapter we reveal the free software no PC owner should be without, and show you how to save power – and money – with your new system. We'll also give you peace of mind by explaining how to make backups and protect your PC from viruses.

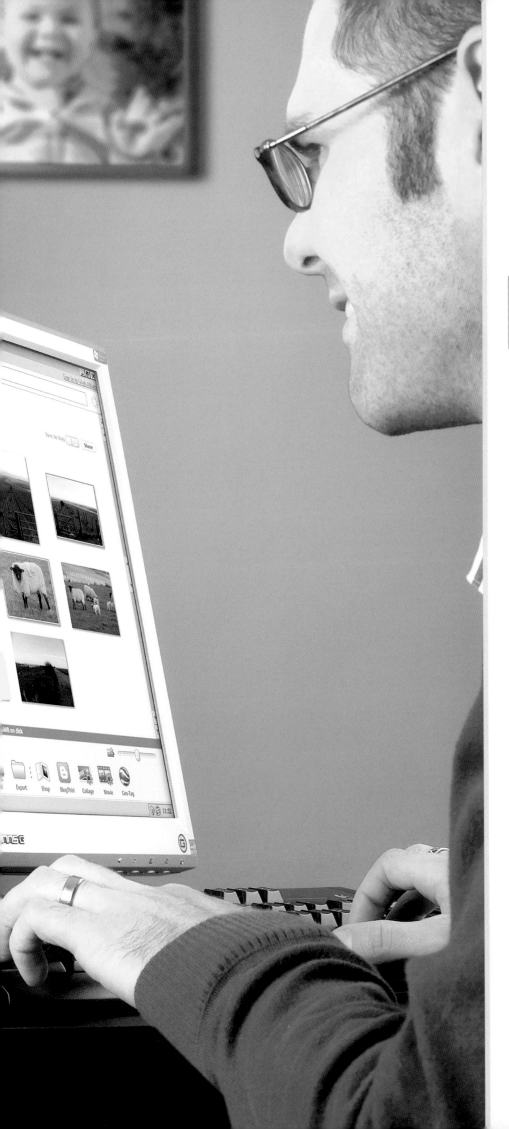

IN THIS CHAPTER

Essential tools	**118**
LibreOffice.org 3	**118**
AVG Anti-Virus Free Edition	**119**
Paint.NET	**119**
Picasa 3	**120**
CDBurnerXP	**120**
Free Download Manager	**121**
Freebyte Backup	**121**
7-Zip	**121**
VLC media player	**121**
Saving power with your new PC	**122**
Creating a backup	**124**
Adding virus protection	**126**

Essential tools

ONCE YOU'VE BUILT your PC and everything is working perfectly, you may feel that your computing experience isn't quite complete. This is because, unlike a Mac OS installation, very little extra software is installed with Windows. You get a primitive word processor called WordPad, an image program called Microsoft Paint, which has barely changed since 1992, and very little else. There's no way to create complicated word-processing documents, do your accounts in a spreadsheet or edit photos.

More importantly, as Windows doesn't come with a virus scanner, you're left wide open to all kinds of internet threats. Windows XP can't even burn files to DVD, and Vista's disc-authoring capabilities leave much to be desired. Both versions also lack a credible alternative to Apple's iPhoto image organiser, although Windows 7 is an improvement .

↑ Microsoft Office 2010 looks great and is very powerful, but it's expensive and most people won't touch half its features. LibreOffice is compatible with Office file formats, and is a credible and free alternative

In the not too distant past, you had to splash out on products such as Microsoft Office, Adobe Photoshop Elements, Norton Internet Security and Roxio Easy Media Creator to make your PC usable. Recently, though, a few software packages have emerged that offer the same features for free. As you'll see, LibreOffice is an impressive office suite, Paint.NET is a powerful image editor, AVG Anti-Virus will keep you safe online and CDBurnerXP lets you burn discs to your heart's content. Furthermore, Google's Picasa will let you organise your photos and share them online.

We've also covered some smaller free utilities that will make your new system easier and more fun to use. The easiest way to install these apps is to use the free automatic installer online at www.ninite.com.

LibreOffice.org
LibreOffice.org 3

DOWNLOAD DETAILS **www.libreoffice.org**
FILE SIZE **130MB**

As far as office software is concerned, a clean installation of Windows will come with an unimpressive word processor and nothing else. Fortunately, you don't have to splash out on the full version of Microsoft Office to give yourself powerful word processor and spreadsheet applications.

LibreOffice.org includes both of these essentials, as well as a presentation program, the Draw vector drawing package and the Base database application. The Writer word processing, Calc spreadsheet and Impress presentation applications are all compatible with Office file formats up to Office 2003, and can open and save documents either in Microsoft's formats or in the suite's OpenDocument format.

There's very little missing from the applications, and most are easy to use. Writer has a spellcheck, and a selection of styles and fonts, as well as word count and table of contents generation features. We can't really see anything missing from what Calc can do, as it supports all the functions and formulas we've ever needed. It even handles charts better than Excel 2007. Impress looks like an older version of PowerPoint, and comes with a couple of different templates

↑ Packed with features, LibreOffice.org is an essential download

to get you started. The last two applications are more niche, but could still be useful. Draw is a reasonable program, but we found it the most fiddly part of the suite to use and it took us a while to master it. Base is a powerful SQL-compatible database, which lets you create searchable linked data tables.

LibreOffice.org may not look as flashy as Microsoft Office 2007, but there's little missing in the way of features and it's free, rather than £167. It's an essential download for every new PC.

AVG Technologies
AVG Anti-Virus
Free Edition

DOWNLOAD DETAILS **http://free.avg.com**

FILE SIZE **47MB**

Even though Microsoft claims that Windows 7 is more secure than any previous version of the operating system, you'd be mad to go online without security software on your PC. A good security suite will protect you against viruses, but will also spot other malware, such as spyware and adware, which can lead to anything from a few annoying pop-ups to your banking logon details being passed on to unscrupulous criminals.

As new viruses and spyware programs are discovered all the time, your security suite needs to be continually updated to maintain the appropriate level of protection. Most security software companies make you pay a subscription to receive the updates, but AVG offers both its software and the subscription for free for non-commercial use. There's no catch, either.

The AVG software includes a virus scanner, which can be set to scan your hard disk at regular intervals, a resident shield that lives in your computer's memory and detects viruses as they appear, an email scanner and a program, which scans links

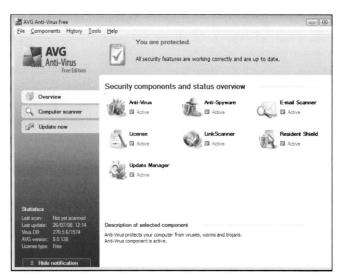

↑ AVG's anti-virus application will help protect your computer

in search engine results to check whether or not they lead to malicious websites. Recently, AVG also added a spyware resident shield, so you're protected against all the threats the internet has to offer.

If you're seriously worried about security threats, consider a paid-for program, such as Kaspersky Internet Security 2009, but AVG Free is certainly a credible home alternative.

Rick Brewster/Ed Harvey
Paint.NET

DOWNLOAD DETAILS **www.getpaint.net**

FILE SIZE **1.5MB**

While Windows has a reasonable image viewer as standard, Microsoft Paint is laughable as an image editor. Adobe Photoshop Elements is our favourite image-editing program, and, at around £50, is fair value. However, a good free alternative is Paint.NET. It's not the only free image-editing application for Windows, as you can also download GIMP from *www.gimp.org*. GIMP's user interface may make your head hurt, though, which is why we prefer Paint.NET.

The program is a tiny download of just 1.5MB, though if you have Windows XP, you'll also need to install Microsoft's .NET framework, which is a free download from *www.microsoft.com*. It has a clean interface that's reminiscent of Photoshop, with floating palettes and information windows. The package supports all the usual image-editing functions, such as layers, cropping and levels and curves adjustments. It also has several image effects as standard. You can save images in most standard formats, including JPEG, BMP, GIF and TIFF, and compressed image settings are handled with a clear preview to show you what your saved image will look like.

It does have a couple of omissions, most notably an Unsharp Mask feature, which is a popular method to sharpen an image.

↑ Paint.NET's clean user interface is reminiscent of Photoshop's

However, the application has an active user community producing plug-ins to use with the software, including an Unsharp Mask plug-in. You will have to search through the forums to find what you need, though.

Paint.NET is astonishing for a free program, and has the advantage of being a small download. It may take you a bit of work and research to add all the features you will need, but it's well worth the effort.

Google
Picasa 3

DOWNLOAD DETAILS http://picasa.google.com

FILE SIZE **6MB**

Picasa 3 is a fantastic photo organisation and editing program from Google. It's a relatively small download, and is easy to install and set up. You should be careful when installing the program that you select the options you want, as by default it'll add shortcuts to your desktop, Quick Launch and System Tray, and set Google as your default search engine.

Picasa will scan your PC for any images when you first run it, read the time data encoded in each photo and arrange your pictures by date. The Library view displays all your photos as thumbnails, and double-clicking on a picture takes you into the editing view. This gives you most of the editing options you'll need to make your photos presentable, such as cropping, red-eye reduction, straightening and contrast and colour adjustment. There are also several effects, including Sharpen, Sepia, Black and White and Soft Focus.

Once you're happy with your pictures, you can view them as a slideshow, with a lovely fade effect between each photo. The best thing about Picasa, though, is its online storage. To use this you'll need a Google Mail account, which you can get at *http://mail.google.com*. Once you have an account, you simply

↑ You can share your pictures online with Picasa 3

select the pictures you want to upload and click the Web Album button. You can upload photos in a quality suitable for viewing in a web browser, or upload bigger files that are good enough to print. Once your photos are online, you can make the album publicly available, or restrict it to only the people you invite to view your pictures. Google gives you 1GB of storage for free, which is enough for around 5,000 photos at web-quality settings. Vista users should try the built-in Windows Photo Gallery first before downloading Picasa, though.

Canneverbe Limited
CDBurnerXP

DOWNLOAD DETAILS http://cdburnerxp.se

FILE SIZE **2.9MB**

Windows 7, Vista and XP all have built-in CD-burning capabilities, and the later versions of the operating system can also burn DVDs, but these applications are fairly primitive and not particularly easy to use. CDBurnerXP is a powerful free program that makes it easy to burn data files to disc, turn audio files into a music CD and create CD and DVD images.

As with Paint.NET (page 119), if you're running Windows XP, you'll need to download and install the .NET Framework to use CDBurnerXP. The program itself is only a small download, and is simple to install.

The main interface will be familiar to anyone who's used a CD-burning program such as Nero. To create a CD, you just need to drag and drop files from the folder view at the top of the screen into your disc compilation at the bottom. You don't have to choose which type of disc you want to burn before you start your compilation, as CDBurnerXP automatically chooses the right file system depending on which type of disc is in the drive.

Once you've created your compilation, you just click the Burn icon to create your disc. You can also select Save

↑ CDBurnerXP makes it easy to burn data files to CD

compilation as ISO file from the File menu to create a disc image to burn later. Usefully, the program also has the option to convert NRG and BIN image files, as used by Nero and some other CD-burning programs, to the more compatible ISO format.

Commercial applications such as Nero and Easy Media Creator have some impressive video disc-authoring features, but for most people CDBurnerXP will be the only disc-burning program they'll need.

DOWNLOAD MANAGER SOFTWARE

Free Download Manager
Free Download Manager

DOWNLOAD DETAILS **www.freedownloadmanager.org**
FILE SIZE **5.6MB**

Essentially, Free Download Manager makes downloading files faster. When you start to download a file, the program splits the file into blocks and downloads all of them simultaneously. We found downloads were often four times faster using this program. You can also pause and resume downloading most files.

The application also has some other powerful features. You can use it to download movies from various video-sharing sites, such as YouTube and Google Video, and you can automatically convert these from the FLV format to more compatible formats such as MPEG4. Free Download Manager can also be used as a BitTorrent client, so is the only program you need to install to take care of all your downloads.

↑ You can download video from sites such as YouTube

BACKUP SOFTWARE

Freebyte.com
Freebyte Backup

DOWNLOAD DETAILS **www.freebyte.com/fbbackup**
FILE SIZE **785KB**

Freebyte Backup is a simple program that lets you back up the contents of your PC's hard disk to an external hard disk. To make a backup, you simply add the drives and directories to be included, then specify any files you want to exclude from the backup, either by the date they were created or by file type. You then just click the Start button and the files you specified will be backed up.

Once you've made your first backup, you can set the software to copy only files that are new or have been changed since the last time you backed up your PC, which drastically cuts down the amount of time the process takes. Automatic backups can be scheduled using the Windows Task Scheduler, although this can be tricky to configure.

↑ Back up your data with Freebyte

ARCHIVE EXTRACTING SOFTWARE

Igor Pavlov
7-Zip

DOWNLOAD DETAILS **www.7-zip.org**
FILE SIZE **1MB**

Even though Windows-supported ZIP files are the most common form of archive, there are many other kinds. 7-Zip can extract the majority of archives, including the popular RAR format, as well as CD and DVD image ISO files.

The program is particularly useful for extracting batches of archives. You simply have to double-click on the files, select Extract and the program will extract each archive's contents into the folder in which the archive is situated. You can also associate, extract or create archives by right-clicking on files in Windows Explorer and using the 7-Zip menu.

7-Zip is an easy way to deal with different types of archive without having to install multiple programs, and it's a tiny download. With the ability to create archives as well as extract them, it's an essential tool, particularly if you regularly download files from the net.

↑ 7-Zip can deal with different types of archive

MEDIA PLAYING SOFTWARE

VideoLAN
VLC media player

DOWNLOAD DETAILS **www.videolan.org**
FILE SIZE **9.3MB**

Playing back audio and video files on a PC can be tricky. Even though all PCs come with Windows Media Player, there are many types of file that it doesn't support, so you'll need to install specific audio and video codecs to play them. Windows XP doesn't even have support for DVD movies as standard.

Finding out which codec is missing from your system can be a tricky business, but VLC takes much of the pain out of this process. It will play most types of audio and video files, including DVDs. It's simple to install, and will launch automatically when you double-click on a compatible file type. It can even play files that are incomplete. With built-in support for DVDs, it's one of the most comprehensive media players and it's completely free. VLC is the simplest way to play back media files.

↑ VLC lets you play DVDs as well as most other media files

Saving power with your new PC

THE RISING COSTS of electricity and increasing concerns over the environment are two very good reasons to consider ways of cutting down on power consumption. PCs are one of the worst offenders in the home, but other devices connected to them, such as printers, monitors and external hard disks, all have their part to play.

Fortunately, there are several things you can do to save power and make your computer more efficient. We'll show you how much power your devices really use, how much it costs you to run them and how to save money by putting your devices into standby mode.

COST OF LIVING

First, it's worth explaining how costs are calculated. Every electrical device draws power, measured in watts (volts x amps). This is the figure used to describe light bulbs – a 100W bulb draws 100W of power. Over an hour this would be a watt

↓ Devices left on can use a huge amount of power, which will cost you a small fortune

hour. Electricity companies then charge your consumption based on the number of kilowatt hours (kWh) you're using. As a kilowatt is 1,000W, you first have to convert the wattage of any measured product into kilowatts by dividing by 1,000. So, a 100W light bulb uses 0.1kW. Over an hour, this would be 0.1kWh. If your electricity company charges you 11p per kWh, your 100W light bulb would cost you 1.1p per hour to run. In reality, most electricity companies use a two-tier system of charging. A fairly common tariff is 14p per kWh for the first 728 kWh per year and then 12p for each kWh thereafter.

For our calculations we've assumed the higher figure of 14kWh. While this means that we've ended up with higher costs overall, it gives us a fair comparison between each device. You can try our Google Docs spreadsheet for calculating running costs by visiting *http://tinyurl.com/powersaver*. You'll need a Google account to access it, but can

↗ Devices such as the Intelliplug can help you save power

DEVICE	POWER WHEN ON	STANDBY POWER	TYPICAL COST PER YEAR*
PC	129W	3W	£40
Laptop	32W	3W	£17
LCD monitor	29W	2W	£8
Inkjet printer	Varies**	3W	£2
Network storage	41W	1W	£34
LCD TV	158W	3W	£33

*We've assumed a typical day's use for each product (eight hours a day for PCs, four hours a day for TVs), using standby modes where appropriate and being turned off at the plug when not in use

**Inkjet printers typically use between 10W and 30W to print a page of paper, but this is for a short amount of time, so the standby power is the biggest factor

sign up for a free one on that web page. Once you've accessed the spreadsheet, select Copy spreadsheet from the File menu to edit it in your own account. All you need to do is set your kWh cost and, for each device, type in its power usage figures, the number of hours a day it's on, off (at the socket) and in standby mode and the sheet will work out the rest.

MEASURING YOUR DEVICES
Measuring electrical devices is easy. All you need is a plug-in power monitor, such as the Plug-In Mains Power and Energy Monitor (£28, *www. maplin.co.uk*). This plugs into your wall socket, and then you just plug the electrical device you want to test into it. The reading on the screen tells you how many watts your device is drawing. Using the calculations above, you can work out how much a device will cost you each year.

You'll be quite surprised at the results. For example, a typical PC uses around 120W when on, while an LCD monitor will use around 29W (149W in total). If you were to leave both on all day every day for a year, you'd be using 1,305kWh per annum, which would cost a staggering £183 a year. However, putting a PC into standby mode means that it uses only around 3W, which is similar to an LCD monitor's 2W in standby mode. Turning them off at the plug when you're not using them would save more money, as you're not drawing any power.

Typically, a computer that's on eight hours a day with no standby modes turned on would cost around £61 a year to run. If you were to set the PC to go into standby mode when not in use for, say, three hours a day, it would cost £47 per annum to run – a saving of around £14 every year. The same can be said of every device that you use. The table

(above) shows typical usage figures for electrical devices you have in your home.

COMBATTING THE PROBLEM
In order to save money, devices need to use less electricity. For PCs, this means adjusting Windows' power-saving settings so it automatically powers down after a period of inactivity. For other devices, you need to power them down when they're not in use. Ideally, you should switch devices off at the plug, because many still draw power when they're in standby mode. For example, the average LCD TV draws 3W when in standby mode. If this was to be left on all year, it would cost you £3.67 every year. That's not a huge amount of money, but multiply this sum for every device you own and it adds up to a small fortune. For computer devices, such as printers, switch them off when you're not using them.

If the thought of having to switch off a plug under a desk sounds like too much hassle, then consider buying a product such as OneClick's Intelliplug (£17 from *www. oneclickpower.co.uk*). This has a master socket for your PC and two slave sockets that get power only when your PC is turned on. It's ideal for your monitor and printer, as they'll be on only when your computer is.

You can try other power-saving techniques, too. For example, if you've got network storage, check to see if there's a sleep mode. Setting your storage to shut down overnight when you won't be using it can save you money every year. Follow this advice for all your electrical kit and you could knock more than £100 off your annual electricity bills.

↑ Measuring how much power your devices use could be a real shock

Creating a backup

Backups can be a tiresome chore, but Windows 7's Backup and Restore utility means you can set it and forget it, safe in the knowledge that your data is protected

WE ALL HAVE files we couldn't bear to lose, from essential work documents to photo albums, music collections and videos. Windows 7's powerful built-in Backup and Restore utility can safeguard your data, and all you need to run it is a spare hard disk, network drive, blank DVD or memory stick.

If you've used Vista's Backup tool or third-party software such as Acronis True Image (*www.acronis. co.uk*), you'll be familiar with how it works. The wizard-based utility takes copies of your chosen files – although, disappointingly, not system or program files – and compresses them all into one smaller file, then stores this in an external location.

When you need to retrieve files, the wizard lets you browse through them and restore them to your hard disk. You also have the advanced option of browsing and restoring backup sets from any other Windows 7 PC, giving you a useful way to manage backups across several systems.

SET UP AND FORGET

When you create a new backup task, Backup and Restore will either attempt to choose your backup files automatically or save and compress every file you select. Whenever the same task is run again, it will only add new or edited files, saving time and

TIP
Third-party backup software generally adds more features and flexibility, especially if you have Windows 7 Home Premium with its more basic functions. Acronis True Image Home 2010, for instance, adds continuous protection for your data and can even migrate all your data and programs from one installation of Windows to another.

disk space. The original file and folder structure is retained, which is vital for organised files such as a music collection.

Backup and Restore includes a comprehensive scheduler, so you can leave it to run automatically. It can be set to run monthly, weekly or even daily. If your PC is off at the specified time, the backup will run as soon as you log back on, and it runs in the background so as not to disrupt your work. Backup and Restore also includes options for managing the storage of backup sets, so you can delete old backups as well as setting the system to only store the most recent full backup if you're short on hard disk space.

TOTAL PROTECTION

Users of Windows 7 Home Premium have a slightly limited version of Backup and Restore, which means you can't back up to a network drive. The Professional and Ultimate editions include this ability. All versions have the ability to image your entire hard disk, so should the worst happen you can boot from the install DVD (or repair disc you create) and restore your system on a new hard disk exactly as it was when it was imaged. It's a brilliant way to protect everything.

Creating a system repair disc gives you an extra line of defence: should things go horribly wrong, you can use it to restore your PC to a working state.

You can see the time of your last backup and if it failed, along with the next scheduled backup time and its contents.

This is the drive to which you're going to back up. Make sure you have enough free space for all your files. If there isn't enough room, click Manage space to free some up.

Windows 7 makes it simple to restore all your backed-up files or specific ones you need to retrieve.

HOW TO...
Back up to an external drive

1 **RUN BACKUP AND RESTORE**

First, open the Start menu, go to All Programs, Maintenance, and click on Backup and Restore. In the window that appears, select Set up backup. You'll be offered a choice of all the storage devices connected to your computer – internal and external hard disks, DVD drives and USB flash drives – as well as a button to choose a network location to back up to if you prefer. We've chosen an external hard disk. Windows will offer to select the files to back up, but you're better off ticking the option to pick your own.

2 **CHOOSE YOUR FILES**

Backup and Restore uses Windows 7's new Libraries, so you can quickly back up files of a particular type. Choose your Music, Pictures and Video libraries as well as the other key user account elements, such as Documents and Favorites. (If you have the patience, you should ideally set up separate backup tasks for media and documents, and run them at different intervals depending on their importance.) Then, if necessary, browse your hard disk and add any other folders you'd like to protect. Finally, choose whether to add a full system image to the backup task. It's a good idea to do this now, when you know your system is working perfectly.

3 **SCHEDULE THE TASK**

Your new backup task will run immediately once it's set up, but you can also schedule it to run daily, weekly or monthly, so you always have a safe copy of your important files. To do this, click on Change schedule. Then choose an appropriate day of the week and pick a time from the dropdown list. The backup task will now automatically begin in the background at the specified time, so you can continue working undisturbed. If your PC is off at the time, it will run next time you log on. Now you've scheduled the task, click Save settings and run backup. It may take anything from a few minutes to several hours, depending on the amount of data involved.

4 **RESTORE YOUR FILES**

If you need to retrieve any files, it's easy to restore them. Open Backup and Restore and choose the Restore option at the bottom. It should show any recent backups, or give you the option to locate one stored elsewhere. Restore the entire backup set (or full disk image), or browse through the files you've previously saved to choose which ones will be restored. Then start the restore process and sit back and wait for your vital files to find their way back to where they should be: safe on your hard disk.

Adding virus protection

Computer viruses and other types of malware can wreak havoc on your new system, so installing effective security software to protect your PC and its data is essential

COMPUTER VIRUSES ARE an unfortunate fact of life, so it's important to understand how they can infect your computer and what you can do to protect yourself. The first point is that, technically, most infections these days aren't caused by viruses but by other types of unwanted software, some of which we'll examine below. So when we're talking about keeping your computer safe, it's clearer to say we're fighting 'malware', a general term for all kinds of malicious software.

WHAT IS MALWARE?

For your PC to be infected with malware, it must execute a piece of programming code designed to deliver an ill effect. For example, you may be browsing the web and see an advert for a free music player. You download the file and double-click it, but instead of installing the software you expected, it installs malware. Congratulations: you've just been tricked by a Trojan (named after the Trojan horse of Greek legend).

You can avoid simple deceptions such as this by keeping your wits about you and not running software from untrusted sources: most web browsers will warn you before downloading executable files for precisely this reason.

But it isn't always that easy. Sometimes, hackers find ways to get your web browser to run malicious code automatically when you visit a website. Simply viewing the page causes your PC to become infected, even if you don't click any links or explicitly download anything. This type of malware is known as a 'drive-by download'.

If you think you can stay safe by steering clear of dodgy sites, think again. Unscrupulous hackers have been known to break into respected websites and plant their malware code on legitimate pages. One famous hack a few years ago saw an official website for the US Super Bowl giving malware to visitors. Drive-bys have also been contained in adverts that reputable sites accepted in good faith.

Perhaps the most alarming category of malware is worms. These programs reach out across the net and use technical tricks to implant themselves in the systems they find. Your PC is at risk from a worm attack any time it's connected to the internet, even when you're not browsing.

↑ Microsoft's free Windows Security Essentials can scour your system and eliminate any trace of malware before it ruins your day

TIP
Some people avoid running security software because they believe it will slow down their system. But most modern security packages are extremely lightweight, consuming only a small amount of memory and placing a tiny load on your computer's CPU. It makes more sense to live with this minor imposition than leave yourself vulnerable to malware attacks.

WHERE DOES MALWARE COME FROM?

In the 1980s and 1990s, most viruses were written by students and hobbyists who wanted to see how far their creations could spread. These days, however, most malware comes from criminal sources with far more nefarious intentions. Some can record your keystrokes and send details back to their creators; if you use online banking or access other confidential information via the internet, the danger is obvious.

Other malware programs subsume your PC into a so-called 'botnet', a network of 'robot' systems that can be controlled remotely by hackers. Botnets are typically used to send spam emails from thousands of locations at once, making the original sender impossible to identify. Being part of a botnet can eat up your computer's resources and clog up your internet connection, as well as inconveniencing other users.

Today's malware creators don't want to create a stir; on the contrary, they want their work to go unnoticed so they can keep harvesting bank details and sending spam. So if your PC is infected, the odds are you won't know about it. That makes it all the more important to avoid infection.

➜ Internet Explorer can't prevent your PC from getting infected, but it can remind you of the risks of downloading software

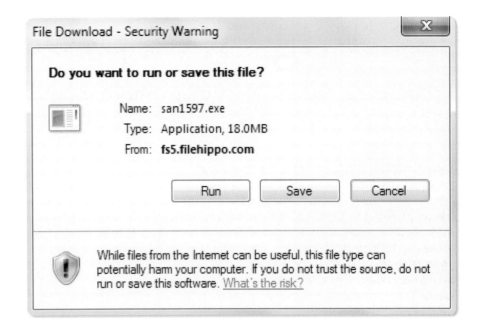

HOW CAN YOU PROTECT YOURSELF?

Many of the technical weaknesses that made previous versions of Windows vulnerable to malware infections possible have been closed in Windows 7, so for the time being you're unlikely to be hit by a drive-by or a worm. However, hackers are sure to find and exploit the inevitable holes in the new operating system. That's why the first step in protecting yourself is to allow Windows Update to install new security enhancements automatically as they become available.

The second step is to pay attention to the User Account Control (UAC) requests that Windows 7 will periodically display. If UAC pops up unexpectedly, warning you that a program is trying to change your system settings, it's a fair bet that something suspicious is happening; you should deny the request and run a malware check.

The third step is to install security software and keep it up to date. The Windows Defender module that's built into Windows 7 can detect some types of malware. Microsoft's free Security Essentials

package detects a much wider range of threats, and can leap in to warn you as soon as any type of malware is recognised on your PC. Ideally, you should consider investing in a third-party security suite, since these have many additional options to keep you safe: we've listed some of the choices available below.

Security software

There are many security packages available for Windows 7; respected brands include Avira, BullGuard, Eset, Kaspersky and Norton. These companies offer antivirus programs that can detect all types of malware using behavioural analysis. That means they don't just look for known malware files; they determine whether a program is good or bad based on the changes it makes to your system. They can therefore protect your PC against new threats that haven't yet been identified.

You can also invest in a more comprehensive security suite, which will include the standard antivirus module plus an enhanced firewall to prevent worms and other intruders getting into your system in the first place. Many packages also add protection against unwanted email, such as spam and phishing messages that try to trick you into giving away passwords and personal information. Some include parental control features, too. All these

features are already built into Windows 7, but independent packages are typically more customisable and offer more features.

PAY UP OR

Security software must be constantly updated in order to recognise ever-evolving threats. Normally, when you buy a security package you'll be entitled to one year of free updates, although there are often reduced rates available if you pay for a number of years up front.

If you don't want to spend any money, there are a number of free options available. Apart from Microsoft's own Security Essentials (available from *www.microsoft.com*), Avira (*www.avira.com*) and AVG (*www.avg.com/uk*) provide effective free antivirus applications. They're not as sophisticated as the paid-for products, but you can use them for as long as you like and benefit from free regular updates.

⬆ Antivirus software isn't included with Windows 7, but there are plenty of third-party packages to choose from, some of which are free for home users

As you might expect, some security suites are better than others, and none can guarantee a 100 per cent success rate. Check independent software reviews, such as those in *Computer Shopper* magazine, to see which suites have a good track record and which might be more likely to let malware slip through the net.

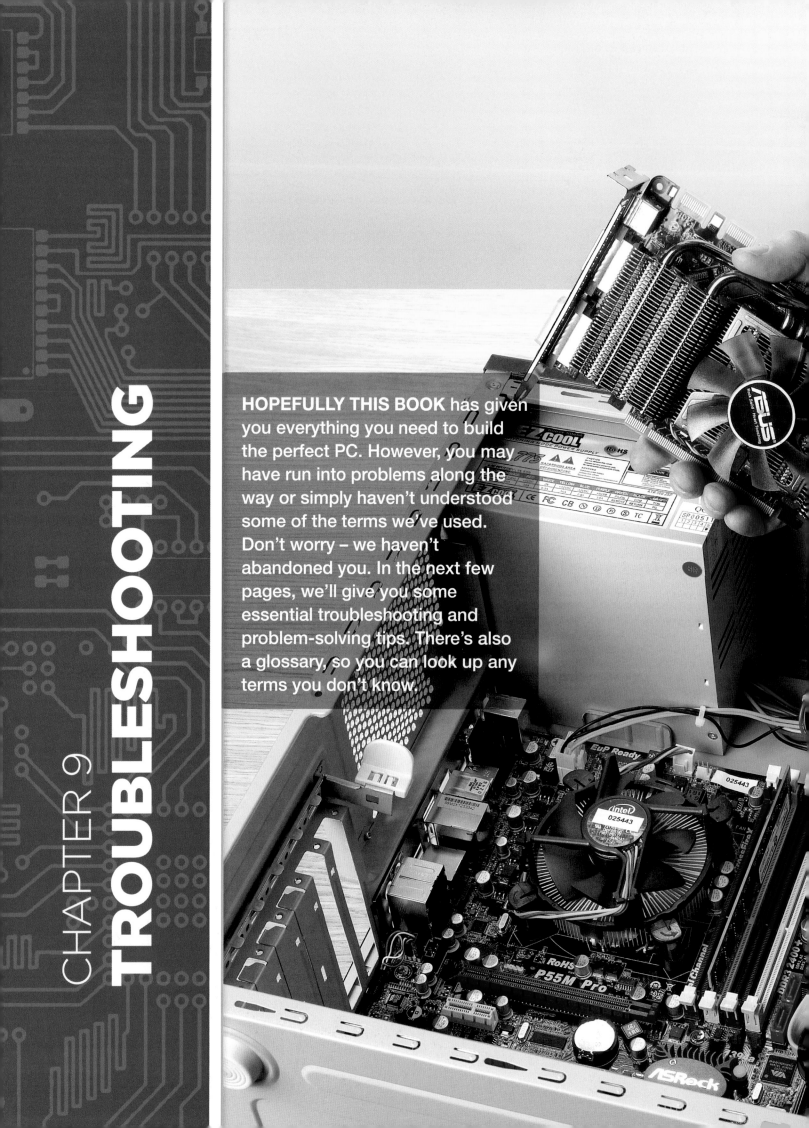

CHAPTER 9
TROUBLESHOOTING

HOPEFULLY THIS BOOK has given you everything you need to build the perfect PC. However, you may have run into problems along the way or simply haven't understood some of the terms we've used. Don't worry – we haven't abandoned you. In the next few pages, we'll give you some essential troubleshooting and problem-solving tips. There's also a glossary, so you can look up any terms you don't know.

IN THIS CHAPTER

Top 10 tips for solving
  boot problems   130

Fixing boot problems   132

BIOS beep codes   134

How to restore your system   135

Windows problems   136

Device Manager   138

Task Manager   140

Event Viewer   142

Top 10 tips for solving
  peripheral problems   144

Solving sound problems   146

Solving monitor problems   148

Testing memory   150

Testing your hard disk   152

Testing your new PC
  for heat   154

Testing your processor   156

Top 10 tips for solving boot problems

If you're having trouble getting Windows to start, these tips will help you get it up and running with the minimum of hassle

THERE ARE MANY reasons why a PC won't boot into its operating system. Many are easy to cure, while others take a little more time.

1 CHECK YOUR USB DEVICES

USB devices are often the cause of PCs refusing to load Windows. The boot sequence appears to be running correctly, but just before you see the Windows splash screen, the PC appears to hang or freeze. You'll either see a black screen, or a white cursor flashing in the top left of the screen. Usually this is caused by USB devices, particularly memory card readers. Check whether you've left a flash drive in a USB port or a memory card in a reader (or digital camera or camcorder) that's connected to your PC. Many printers also have memory card readers. Remove any cards and press your PC's reset button to reboot it.

2 CHECK FOR OPTICAL DISCS

It's easy to leave a bootable CD or DVD in a drive accidentally. This could cause your PC to refuse to boot, or to boot into an application other than your operating system. It may not be obvious that your PC is booting from an optical disc, so check that your drives are empty and reboot.

3 CHECK THE BOOT ORDER

BIOS settings are critical for booting, so if your OS isn't starting properly or you're getting some odd messages, you should enter the BIOS and check the boot sequence. When you see the POST screen, press Del (some computers will require you to press F2, F10 or F12, but most display a message telling you which key to press). Look for an Advanced BIOS Options menu and a Boot Sequence menu within that. Ensure that the primary boot device is the hard disk that has your operating system on it. If you have more than one hard disk and don't know which one Windows is on, you may have to try setting each as the primary device and rebooting to see if it fixes the problem. CD-ROM and floppy drives can boot before the hard disk, but this will slow the boot time down.

4 LISTEN FOR STRANGE NOISES

Listen for any unusual noises coming from your PC. As your PC boots, you should hear

↓ Make sure you disconnect any USB devices if Windows isn't loading properly

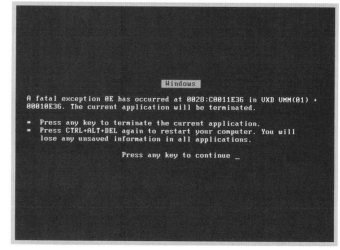

↑Overheating can cause the dreaded blue screen of death

↑ Check the boot order in the BIOS if your computer isn't booting properly

flurries of clicking from the hard disk, but if there's a rhythmic scraping or chirping noise, your hard disk may have failed. In this case, you'll need to restore a backup to a new disk.

↑ Check the power cables if your graphics card is emitting a high-pitched noise

5 CHECK YOUR CABLES

Make sure that no cables have become dislodged. Start with power cables and both ends of your monitor's cable. If you don't find any problems, remove your PC's side panel and check internal cables, particularly the hard disk's power and data cables. Many modern graphics cards require one or two power cables, so check these are properly connected. Without a power cable, some graphics cards emit a high-pitched noise.

6 RESET THE BIOS

Overclocking can cause boot problems, so you should check your motherboard's manual to see if there's a way to boot the PC at standard speeds without losing all your BIOS settings. If not, you'll need to reset the BIOS (this is also known as resetting the CMOS). The same manual should document the procedure, which usually involves moving a motherboard jumper to a reset position, although in rare cases you may find a switch or button on the outside of the PC.

7 CHECK FOR OVERHEATING

Your PC may be overheating and it may fail to boot after an unexplained 'blue screen'. Wait for at least 30 minutes to allow the components to cool down and try turning on the PC again. Meanwhile, investigate potential reasons for overheating, such as a broken fan. You should ensure that your PC isn't placed next to a heat source such as a radiator.

8 BEEP, BEEP!

If your PC is making an unusual beeping noise, you'll need to refer to your motherboard manual to diagnose the problem. If you don't have a manual, we've provided a list of common BIOS

beep codes on page 134. Some motherboards have LED displays that you can use along with the descriptions of each code in the manual to determine the status of the POST sequence. These often make it much simpler to solve the problem as you can see precisely how far the PC makes it through the boot process before failing. Knowing this information should make it obvious which component is causing the problem.

9 CHECK HARDWARE AND SOFTWARE

If you've recently installed a piece of hardware and you see a blue screen when your PC boots, the cause is probably the new hardware. Uninstall it and see if it fixes the problem. It could also be caused by new software, so try and boot into Safe Mode by pressing F8 repeatedly after the initial POST screen. It's also worth noting that you'll probably see a blue screen if you've recently swapped the hard disk for one from a different PC and tried to boot from it.

10 UNPLUG YOUR HARDWARE

If none of the tips above has helped you solve the problem, you should disconnect any unnecessary hardware. All a PC needs to show a POST message is a motherboard, a processor, one memory module, a graphics card and a power supply. All other hardware can be unplugged. If the PC now boots, begin reconnecting other components one at a time until the problem returns. If it still doesn't boot, it's likely to be a hardware failure. At this point, it's worth trying to borrow components known to be working, and swapping them with yours to find out which of the core parts is defective.

Fixing boot problems

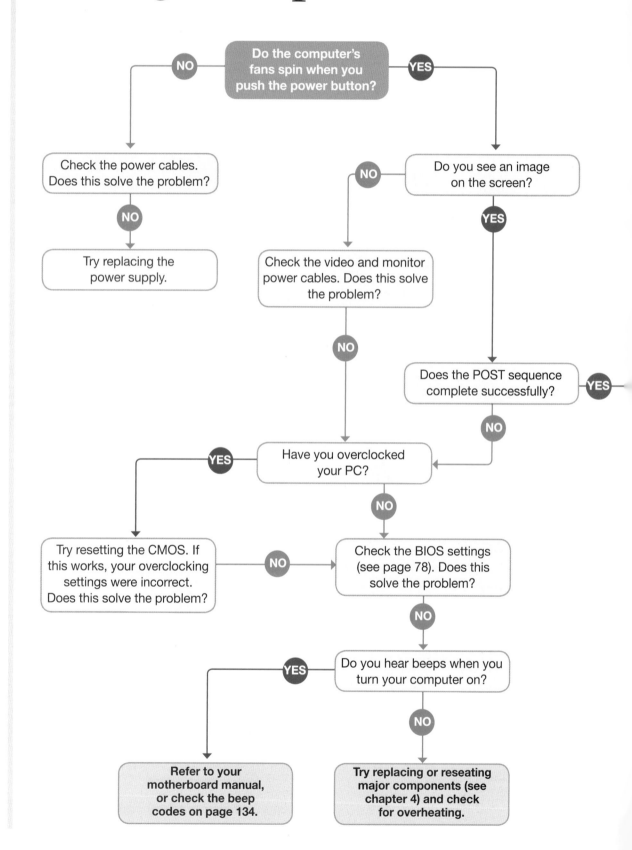

Do the computer's fans spin when you push the power button?

NO → Check the power cables. Does this solve the problem?

NO → Try replacing the power supply.

YES → Do you see an image on the screen?

NO → Check the video and monitor power cables. Does this solve the problem?

YES → Does the POST sequence complete successfully?

YES →

NO →

Check the video and monitor power cables → NO → Have you overclocked your PC?

YES → Try resetting the CMOS. If this works, your overclocking settings were incorrect. Does this solve the problem?

NO → Check the BIOS settings (see page 78). Does this solve the problem?

NO → Do you hear beeps when you turn your computer on?

YES → Refer to your motherboard manual, or check the beep codes on page 134.

NO → Try replacing or reseating major components (see chapter 4) and check for overheating.

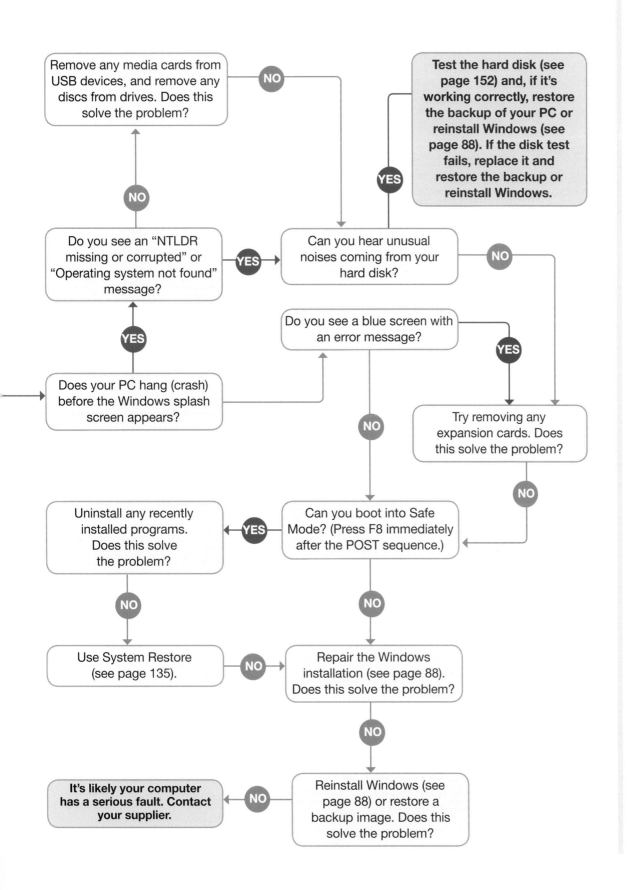

Remove any media cards from USB devices, and remove any discs from drives. Does this solve the problem?

NO

NO

Test the hard disk (see page 152) and, if it's working correctly, restore the backup of your PC or reinstall Windows (see page 88). If the disk test fails, replace it and restore the backup or reinstall Windows.

YES

Do you see an "NTLDR missing or corrupted" or "Operating system not found" message?

YES

Can you hear unusual noises coming from your hard disk?

NO

YES

Do you see a blue screen with an error message?

YES

NO

Does your PC hang (crash) before the Windows splash screen appears?

Try removing any expansion cards. Does this solve the problem?

NO

Uninstall any recently installed programs. Does this solve the problem?

YES

Can you boot into Safe Mode? (Press F8 immediately after the POST sequence.)

NO

NO

Use System Restore (see page 135).

NO

Repair the Windows installation (see page 88). Does this solve the problem?

NO

It's likely your computer has a serious fault. Contact your supplier.

NO

Reinstall Windows (see page 88) or restore a backup image. Does this solve the problem?

BIOS beep codes

If your PC makes a beeping noise when it boots, it may be trying to send you a message. Here's how to interpret the noises

WHEN YOU SWITCH on or reset your PC it performs a diagnostic test called a Power-On Self Test (POST) to check that all the components are present and working correctly. First, it checks core components such as the system clock, processor, RAM, keyboard controller and graphics card. If any device fails this part of the POST, you'll hear a series of beeps from the PC. After the graphics card has passed its test, the BIOS can then indicate any errors onscreen, such as the classic "Keyboard error or no keyboard present. Press F1 to continue" message.

Beep codes differ depending on the BIOS manufacturer, but here are some common codes for popular BIOSes.

AMI BIOS
- **ONE BEEP** All OK
- **TWO BEEPS** Memory parity error (reseat or replace memory)
- **THREE BEEPS** Memory read or write error (reseat or replace memory)
- **FOUR BEEPS** Motherboard timer problem (replace motherboard)
- **FIVE BEEPS** Processor or memory error (reseat or replace processor and memory)
- **SIX BEEPS** Keyboard controller failure (replace motherboard)
- **SEVEN BEEPS** Processor exception interrupt error (reseat or replace processor)
- **EIGHT BEEPS** Display memory read or write failure (reseat or replace graphics card)

- **NINE BEEPS** ROM checksum error (replace BIOS chip or motherboard)
- **10 BEEPS** CMOS shutdown read or write error (replace BIOS chip or motherboard)
- **11 BEEPS** Bad cache memory (replace cache memory if possible)
- **ONE LONG, THREE SHORT BEEPS** Memory error (reseat or remove any memory recently added and reseat all other memory)
- **ONE LONG, EIGHT SHORT BEEPS** Graphics card error (reseat graphics card)

AWARD BIOS
- **ONE LONG, TWO SHORT BEEPS** Graphics card error (reseat or replace graphics card)
- **ONE LONG, THREE SHORT BEEPS** No graphics card, or graphics memory error (install or replace graphics card)
- **TWO SHORT BEEPS** Memory error (reseat or replace memory)
- **ONE HIGH-PITCHED BEEP** Processor overheating
- **ONE HIGH-PITCHED BEEP, ONE LOW-PITCHED BEEP** Processor error

PHOENIX BIOS
Phoenix BIOSes produce a series of beeps separated by a pause. For example:
beep… beep beep beep… beep… beep would be 1-3-1-1
- **1-1-4-1** Level 2 cache error (reseat or replace the processor)
- **1-2-2-3** BIOS ROM checksum (replace BIOS chip or motherboard)
- **1-3-1-1** Memory refresh test failure (reseat or replace memory)
- **1-3-1-3** Keyboard controller failure (replace the motherboard)
- **1-3-4-1** Memory failure (reseat or replace memory)
- **1-3-4-3** Memory refresh test failure (reseat or replace memory)
- **1-4-1-1** Memory refresh test failure (reseat or replace memory)
- **2-1-2-3** BIOS error (replace BIOS chip or motherboard)
- **2-2-3-1** IRQ problem (remove expansion cards or replace motherboard)

HOW TO...
Restore your system

If you're having problems, System Restore – which is built into Windows – allows you to return your PC to a working state

1 TURN ON SYSTEM RESTORE

First, press the Windows-Break keys. Click the System Protection link. Make sure that the C drive has the Protection option set to On. If it doesn't, select drive C, click Configure, select 'Restore system settings and previous versions of files' and click OK.

There must be at least 200MB of free space on your hard disk for System Restore to work. If there isn't, you'll need to clear out unwanted files.

Use the slider to specify how much disk space System Restore is allowed to use; the more it has, the more restore points it can keep.

2 CREATE A RESTORE POINT

Every time you make a significant change to your system, such as installing a new application, Windows automatically creates a restore point. It's good practice to create a restore point manually before you make any changes, though, so you know that you have something to fall back on.

To create a restore point, press Windows-Break and click the System Protection link. Click the Create button, type in a name for the restore point and click OK.

3 RESTORE YOUR SYSTEM

When your PC has a problem, you can revert to any saved restore point. If you know which software is causing the problem, remove it using Uninstall a Program. If it's a driver, turn off your PC and remove the relevant hardware, too. Next, with your PC running, open System Restore from the Start menu. Click Next and Windows 7 will choose a restore point automatically, but you can select a different one from the list if you wish. Pay close attention to the date: use the latest point when you're sure the system worked properly. Allow the restore to finish and your PC to restart.

4 EMERGENCY RESTORE

If something has gone really wrong, your PC may not even boot into Windows. While the PC is booting, keep pressing F8. Instead of the normal Windows startup routine, you'll be offered a menu. Choose Safe Mode with command prompt. Log on as an administrator, and at the command prompt type c:\windows\system32\restore\rstrui.exe (in Vista, type c:\windows\system32\rstrui.exe). This starts System Restore, and you can then choose a restore point to go back to.

Windows problems

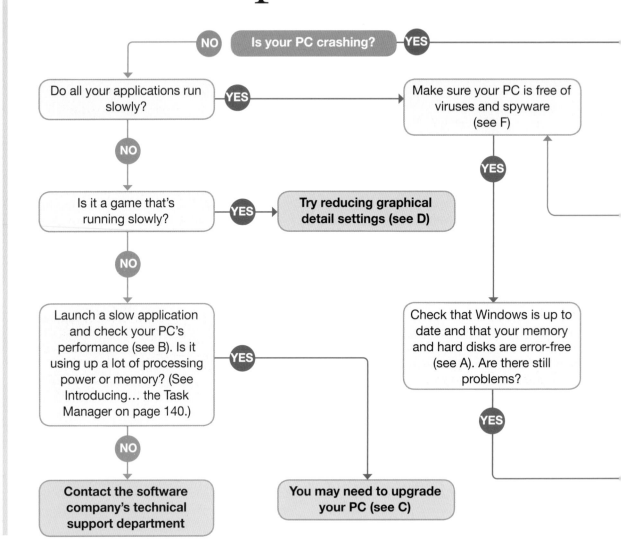

NO — Is your PC crashing? — **YES**

Do all your applications run slowly? — **YES** → Make sure your PC is free of viruses and spyware (see F)

NO

Is it a game that's running slowly? — **YES** → **Try reducing graphical detail settings (see D)**

NO

Launch a slow application and check your PC's performance (see B). Is it using up a lot of processing power or memory? (See Introducing… the Task Manager on page 140.) — **YES**

NO

YES →

Check that Windows is up to date and that your memory and hard disks are error-free (see A). Are there still problems?

YES

Contact the software company's technical support department

You may need to upgrade your PC (see C)

THE A TO G OF FIXING YOUR PC

A Test your memory using Memtest, which you can download for free (see page 150). If it finds any errors, you may need to replace some of your PC's RAM. Contact your PC's technical support line. It's also worth checking that your hard disk has no errors by using the error-checking tool in Windows. Just right-click on the drive, choose Properties and click the Tool tab. Press the Check Now button.

Finally, make sure that Windows has the latest updates. Open Automatic Updates in the Windows Security Center, which is available in the Control Panel.

B If an application is running slowly, it's worth finding out how much of your computer's processing power and memory it is using.

Close all your other applications and press Ctrl-Alt-Del simultaneously to open the Windows Task Manager (see page 140). In the Processes tab you'll be able to see what percentage of your processor power and how much memory (divide by 1,000 for a rough figure in megabytes) each program is using. If it's hogging all the processing power or most of your RAM and is still slow, your PC is struggling

with this program.

C If your application needs more system resources, you may need to upgrade your PC. If you're short on memory, an upgrade is relatively simple. Check your manual to see what kind of memory your PC accepts or go to www. crucial.com and use the online system scanner.

D Modern games can be incredibly demanding. If your graphics card is struggling, it will produce a low frame rate,

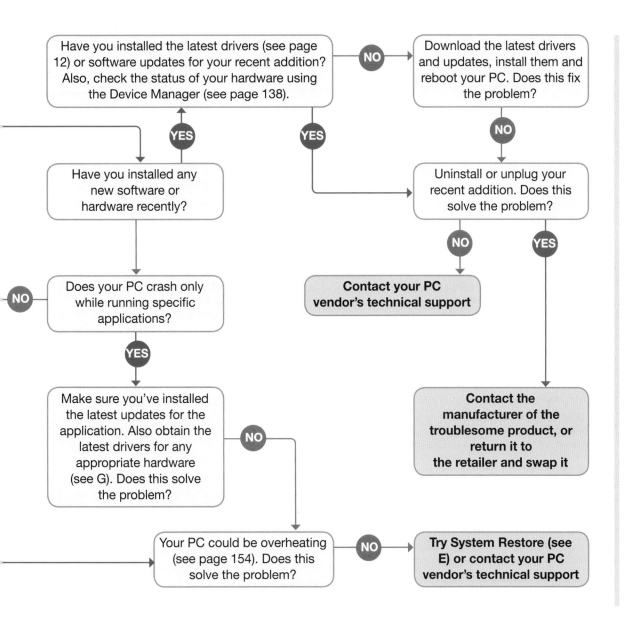

Have you installed the latest drivers (see page 12) or software updates for your recent addition? Also, check the status of your hardware using the Device Manager (see page 138).

NO → Download the latest drivers and updates, install them and reboot your PC. Does this fix the problem?

YES ↓

Have you installed any new software or hardware recently?

YES ↓

NO → Does your PC crash only while running specific applications?

NO → Uninstall or unplug your recent addition. Does this solve the problem?

NO → **Contact your PC vendor's technical support**

YES ↓

Make sure you've installed the latest updates for the application. Also obtain the latest drivers for any appropriate hardware (see G). Does this solve the problem?

YES → **Contact the manufacturer of the troublesome product, or return it to the retailer and swap it**

NO → Your PC could be overheating (see page 154). Does this solve the problem?

NO → **Try System Restore (see E) or contact your PC vendor's technical support**

which causes the game to pause and stutter. Run the game and find the graphics settings in the options menu. Try turning off anti-aliasing (AA) and anisotropic filtering (AF) first to see if this improves your frame rate. If not, reduce the resolution to 1,024x768 or lower.

Make sure that you have the latest patches for your game and the latest drivers for your graphics card by going to Nvidia's or ATI's website, or check your laptop manufacturer's site if you have built-in graphics.

E Your PC keeps a record of any changes made to its settings. If you encounter a problem, you can restore the settings from an earlier date. In Windows 7, the System Restore tool is under Programs, Accessories, System Tools. Alternatively, you can simply type System Restore into the search box. Follow the instructions to restore your PC to the state it was in before your problem started.

F Slow performance may be a sign that your PC is running some undesirable software. This can include such nasties as

viruses, privacy-invading spyware and aggravating advertising pop-ups. These programs can be grouped together under the term malicious software (or malware, for short).

Run a virus scan to find any malware on your PC. If you don't have anti-virus software, download AVG Free Edition from http://free.avg.com and run a full scan.

G If certain types of program such as games cause your PC to crash, check that you have the latest drivers for any hardware that's responsible for running

Introducing...
Device Manager

THE DEVICE MANAGER allows you to view all the hardware inside your computer. It's also the place to go when you're having problems with hardware, as it can help diagnose faults and update device drivers. To open the Device Manager, go to the Control Panel, Hardware and Sound, Device Manager.

You can launch the Device Manager in different ways: it's quicker to right-click on My Computer, then Properties, then Device Manager.

DEVICE SQUAD

You may never have visited the Device Manager before, as there's usually no reason to. When you install a piece of new hardware, you'll also install

any drivers from CD. This process automatically copies files to the appropriate places and the hardware is added to the Device Manager list.

Although you can enable and disable hardware from the Device Manager, it's often more convenient to do so from other places in Windows. The same is true for updating drivers. While you can manually initiate a driver update from an item's properties page in the Device Manager, there's usually no need to, since most drivers downloaded from manufacturers' websites automatically remove old versions and install the new ones.

However, when your hardware stops working as it should or you can't automatically update drivers, the Device Manager comes into its own. The

1 The name of your computer is shown at the top of the tree

2 Click the + symbol next to each category to show the devices within

3 This PC has three disk drives connected: a USB flash drive, a memory card reader and an internal hard disk. The former two are also listed under the Portable Devices heading default view of devices by type shows a collapsed tree structure, where just the headings are shown, but it will automatically expand any category that contains a problem. You may see a yellow exclamation mark next to a component's name, or an arrow pointing downwards. The exclamation mark might mean that the hardware drivers aren't installed, or that the hardware itself cannot start. An arrow denotes that the hardware is disabled.

For this example we'll assume that your Windows desktop is showing enormous icons and you can't adjust the resolution in the Display Settings dialog.

1 OPEN THE DEVICE MANAGER
Scan down the Device Manager list until you come to the Display adapters entry. Click the + symbol, and you should see an exclamation mark, which means the drivers aren't installed. If there's no Display adapters entry, look for Other devices, which should have Unknown device listed.

2 CHECK THE DRIVER
Right-click on this, or on the name of the

graphics card, and choose Properties. Click on the Driver tab and you'll see details of the currently installed driver, if there is one. You may see Microsoft listed next to Driver Provider, but you should install the latest driver from your graphics card manufacturer, such as Nvidia, AMD or Intel.

3 DOWNLOAD THE NEW DRIVER
Visit the appropriate manufacturer's website to obtain the latest driver and download it. If necessary, unzip it into a folder on your hard disk. If the file is a self-executable – ending in .exe – you can run it at this point. If not, return to the Properties page you navigated to in Step 2, and click the Update Driver… button. Click the Browse my computer for driver software button.

4 INSTALL THE DRIVER
Click the Browse… button on the next window that appears. Navigate to the folder where you unzipped the drivers and click Next. Windows should install the drivers, and you may see the screen flicker during the process. You may also have to reboot your PC to finalise the installation.

Introducing... Task Manager

WHEN YOU ENCOUNTER a problem in Windows, your first stop should almost always be the Task Manager. This allows you to shut applications down, view system information – such as the load under which the processor and memory are working – and much more besides.

The Task Manager is particularly useful for identifying troublesome applications or services that are hogging your PC's resources, such as memory or processor time, and slowing it down. It can also help you monitor the size of Windows' page file, as well as keep tabs on network activity.

1 The Applications tab lets you view which applications are running, and allows you to shut them down

2 The Processes tab shows a detailed list of all your programs

3 Vista's Services tab allows you to start, stop and configure system services such as Task Scheduler and WiFi configuration

4 The performance tab shows graphs of processor load and memory usage

The fastest way to open the Task Manager in all versions of Windows is to press the Ctrl-Shift-Esc keys at the same time. A window will open that sits on top of any existing windows, and will remain that way until you either minimise or close it.

The first tab shows the list of running applications. This is useful when an application won't shut down, as you can highlight it in the list and click the End Task button. If the application has crashed and you've been unable to save your work, forcing it to end will probably cause any changes since you last saved the file to be lost, unless the application has an auto-save or auto-recovery feature. For this reason, it's sometimes best to wait for programs that are not responding to come back to life rather than forcing them to quit. Any more than a few minutes of non-responsiveness, however, probably indicates that a program really has crashed.

PART OF THE PROCESS

The Processes tabs lists which programs are running in much greater detail, showing memory and processor usage. Processes using an unusually high amount of the processor or memory may be malfunctioning and may need to be ended and restarted. In many cases, an application listed in the Applications tab will translate to several processes, and you'll sometimes need to use the Processes tab when you can't end a program from the Applications tab. It can be difficult to determine what a process does, but Windows 7's Task Manager additionally shows a description of the process, although you may have to scroll right or expand the Description column to see it fully.

You can sort the list of processes by any column. A useful way to do this is by Owner. You'll see your username, plus any other users currently logged on, and 'system', which is the operating system's processes. You should be able to end any processes next to a username without a problem, except that the program or service will no longer function until you restart it or reboot. Ending system processes is more dangerous, as you might cause Windows to crash or stop working properly. However, the worst that will happen is you'll need to reboot your computer.

The beauty of the Processes tab is that you can choose additional columns of information. From the View menu, choose Select Columns... and you'll see a list of options. We'd recommend ticking I/O reads and I/O writes, as this shows which processes are thrashing the hard disk and memory. Any process that is constantly reading and/or writing could have a problem, and you should investigate it further by finding out what the process is for.

Next is the Services tab. This is similar to the Processes tab, and lists each service's process ID (PID) which is often included in error messages. This can often help you identify troublesome services and end them.

The Performance tab shows several graphs: one for each processor core and one for page file usage. On the left you can see the current processor and page file usage.

If either of these is very high, it could explain why Windows is running slowly. The reason could be because you're running a demanding application or an application has crashed. If youleave your computer in Sleep mode rather thanturning it off, the page file size will build up andslow Windows down. A reboot should fix this issue.

↑ You can see how much bandwidth is being used in the Networking tab

Introducing...
Event Viewer

THE EVENT VIEWER presents detailed system logs, which are special files that record significant events that happen on your computer, such as when an application encounters an error or when the computer enters a standby power state.

The Event Viewer is similar to an aeroplane's black box recorder. It lets you see a summary of your PC's health, and can help you pinpoint which application has caused a problem, as well as providing error codes that can be useful for Google searches.

To launch Event Viewer, either type it into Vista's search bar, or right-click on Computer in the Start menu and choose Manage. Event Viewer is the second item in the System Tools list.

FINDING YOUR WAY AROUND

Although the Event Viewer is designed to be user-friendly, it can still be daunting for many people. It's really designed to assist technicians diagnose faults, but even the non-technical can glean useful information from it.

1 The Overview and Summary panel lets you see at a glance the number of errors and warnings

2 You can jump quickly to any of the logs using the tree in the left pane

3 The Actions pane on the right-hand side of the Event Viewer lets you quickly create custom views, as well as changing the view and refreshing the overview. Actions are context-sensitive, and change depending on the current view

↑ The detailed information on each error can help you diagnose problems

If you know a particular application isn't working as it should, you can search for it in the Application log, which is listed under Windows Logs on the left. Let's say that Google's Updater application isn't working. Click on Application beneath Windows Logs and the listing will appear in the middle pane. You can scroll down the list until you see Google Update in the Source column. Highlight the event and you'll see the error details in the pane below. You may have to resize the window to see the full width of the description as it doesn't automatically wrap the text to fit.

The general description should explain the nature of the error; for example, a required component wasn't found or the installation is corrupted. In this case, reinstalling the application should fix the problem. You may also see a particular filename mentioned, which may help to identify the problem, and an error code, such as

Error: 0x80072ee2. Copying and pasting this into Google along with the application name may shed more light on the problem if the description doesn't make it obvious what you should do next.

SYSTEM LOG

The System log covers operating system events, and can be useful for diagnosing problems with hardware drivers. For example, your PC may be refusing to go into sleep mode or refusing to wake up from it. The System log may show warnings such as 'Display driver nvlddmnkm stopped responding'. This could indicate that it's your graphics card driver causing the problem, and that updating the driver may cure it.

Most of the log will likely contain Information entries, which tell you when services started and stopped. They may also give warnings, such as the one shown in the screen below: "Windows cannot store Bluetooth authentication codes on the local adapter. Bluetooth keyboards might not work in the system BIOS during startup." Again, this can explain why certain problems are occurring.

CUSTOM VIEWS

You can create custom views in the Event Viewer, which allow you to see relevant information more easily, instead of having to wade through thousands of entries in each log. To create a custom view, click Create Custom View… in the right-hand pane of the Event Viewer. You can then select what time period the view should cover, which event types to include, and how to filter them, whether by log or by source.

A simple custom view could filter the errors and warnings from the application and system logs over the previous 24 hours. When you name and save the custom view, it will appear in the Custom Views section in the left-hand pane.

↓ Creating custom views is a good way of keeping track of relevant information

↑ This alert warns that Bluetooth keyboards may not work in the BIOS

Top 10 tips for solving peripheral problems

1 CHECK ALL CABLES
We've said it before, but it bears repeating: check your cables. Whatever problem you're having with your peripheral, make sure the cables are properly connected at both ends and that they're not damaged. If something won't turn on at all, check the fuse in the plug, as these do fail occasionally. Keep a couple of 3A and 13A fuses to hand so you can quickly swap out a suspect fuse.

2 TRY ANOTHER USB PORT
When USB peripherals aren't working properly or aren't being correctly detected by Windows, try unplugging the cable and plugging it into a different USB port. This forces Windows to redetect the hardware and reinstall the drivers, and often solves annoying problems.

If a peripheral isn't behaving properly, check if it's plugged into a USB hub. If it is, disconnect it and reconnect it to a port on your PC or laptop, as some devices, including Apple iPods, don't like being connected via a USB hub.

3 DRY IT OUT
If you accidentally spill liquid on any of your peripherals, unplug all their cables immediately. Place them somewhere hot and dry, such as an airing cupboard, for at least 24 hours to allow them to dry out. There's no guarantee this will save them, but it often works. If you spill a sticky liquid on a peripheral, don't be tempted to pour extra water on to flush it out – this could cause more damage. If it fails to work after the drying out

process, try disassembling it. Most warranties won't cover damage caused by spillages (but check first), so you have nothing to lose by disassembling a peripheral. Remote controls often benefit from being taken apart, as liquid can be trapped between the rubber membrane and the circuit board, preventing buttons from working.

4 PS/2 WARNING
Don't forget that PS/2 peripherals aren't hot-pluggable. If you forget to connect a PS/2 keyboard or mouse to your PC and you only realise when you see an error message during the POST sequence or when the device doesn't work in Windows, don't plug it in. Turn the PC off first, and then connect it, even if it means holding down the power button after booting into Windows. You won't cause any damage to Windows.

5 USE THE RIGHT PORT
A classic mistake is to reach behind your PC to plug in a USB device without looking and inadvertently insert it into the Ethernet port. USB plugs are exactly the same width as a network socket, which means it feels like you've inserted the USB cable correctly as the plug is held tightly in place. It's only when Windows refuses to detect the device that you're aware something's not working properly.

6 KNOW YOUR COLOURS
The same goes for audio connections, as sound cards tend to use minijack sockets for

↑ Make sure video cables are screwed in securely

↑ Know your sound card colours

↑ If you're having webcam problems, ensure your camera is properly selected in the application you're using it with

↑ Eject your USB disks before unplugging them to avoid losing files

everything and rarely have labels next to them. Here's a quick guide to the colour coding:

Green Main stereo output, usually used for front speakers or headphones
Pink Stereo microphone input
Light blue Stereo line input
Black Rear surround speakers
Orange Centre speaker and subwoofer output
Grey Middle surround speakers for 7.1 systems

7 CHECK WEBCAM SETTINGS

If you're having problems with your webcam, such as a lack of video, check the settings of the program that's using it (usually this will be an instant-messaging application such as Windows Live Messenger). Look for a webcam settings option in the menus and make sure you select the webcam from the list of video devices when asked.

If you don't see the make and model of the webcam listed, it may be because the drivers aren't properly installed. If reinstalling the latest drivers from the manufacturer's website doesn't solve the problem, try rebooting your PC and plugging the webcam into a different USB port.

8 ELIMINATING ECHOES

It's common to have problems with webcam audio. If you're using the webcam's built-in microphone, make sure it's selected correctly in a similar way to the video in tip 7. If you hear an echo through your speakers during a web chat, try turning the microphone level down and asking the other person to turn their speaker volume down. If the problem persists, try wearing headphones or a headset with a microphone, as this will eliminate the feedback loop.

9 CRT WARNING

Don't attempt to fix your monitor by opening it up. This is an important safety tip. There are high voltages inside a monitor, and you could seriously injure yourself, even if the monitor has been unplugged from the mains. Whatever component might need replacing, it's almost always more cost-effective to replace the monitor with a new one. You'll probably end up with a better-quality monitor and a higher resolution in the process.

10 AVOID DATA LOSS

Eject your USB storage devices rather than just removing them. It's a pain ejecting a flash drive or memory card when you want to remove it from your PC, especially as it may seem to do no harm. However, if you pull it out before Windows has finished writing files to it (and this can happen a while after you save a document, due to Windows' delayed writes policy) you could easily lose work or corrupt files on the USB device. If Windows' eject method is too inconvenient, install a program that allows you to remove USB devices quickly, such as the free USB Disk Ejector, which you can download from *http://quick.mixnmojo.com/usb-disk-ejector*.

← Don't attempt to open up and repair a monitor yourself – there are dangerous voltages inside

Solving sound problems

IT'S A FAMILIAR situation: you turn on your computer and fire up your media player to listen to some music. The file appears to play, but there's no sound coming from your speakers. It's a common and frustrating problem, but is usually easy to fix.

First, check the obvious. Are your speakers switched on and the volume turned up? Are the audio cables correctly connected to your PC? If you have a laptop, does it have a mute button, or a Function key combination that allows you to mute and unmute the sound?

Next, check whether the sound is muted within Windows. You may see an icon that looks like a speaker cone in the Notification Area at the bottom of your desktop. If not, click the < button to expand the view to see all icons. Single-click on the speaker and you should see a volume slider and a Mute tickbox. Ensure that the box isn't ticked and that the volume slider isn't set to minimum. If you don't see an icon, click Start, All Programs, Control Panel. Click on the Hardware and Sound link, then Sound to launch the dialog box for all sound controls.

MULTIPLE SOUND DEVICES

Another common reason for hearing no sound is because you have multiple audio devices connected to or installed on your computer. For example, you may have recently installed a Skype handset or headset. In effect, this is a sound card in itself, and Windows can inadvertently make this the primary sound device, meaning that all sounds, whether from Windows Media Player, Internet

Explorer or another application, are being routed to the handset instead of your speakers. You can either unplug the device, which should fix the problem instantly, or you can select a different audio device in the Control Panel.

Navigate to the sound properties in the Control Panel as described above. In Windows 7, there are separate tabs for Playback and Recording, allowing you to select different devices for each option very easily. Click on the Playback option, right-click on the audio device you want to use and click 'Set as default'. If the device is greyed out you will first need to right-click on it and select Enable.

If this doesn't solve the problem, you may need to check your sound card's audio mixer, which provides volume controls for different devices, such as the microphone, line-in and WAV. To open the mixer, click on the speaker icon in the Notification Area and click the Mixer link.

DEVICE MANAGER

If you still have no joy, check that the sound card is working properly by opening Device Manager (see page 138). Scroll down the list of hardware until you come to Sound, video and game controllers. Expand the tree by clicking the + symbol, and look for any yellow exclamation marks or red crosses. Exclamation marks mean there's a problem with

↓ Make sure the volume sliders aren't set to zero and that they're not muted

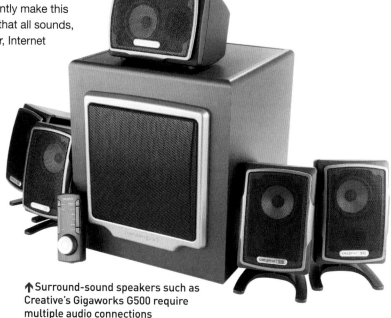

↑ Surround-sound speakers such as Creative's Gigaworks G500 require multiple audio connections

→ Skype handsets can play havoc with your audio settings

↑ Most sound cards have lots of identical-looking minijack inputs and outputs

the hardware – drivers may not be correctly installed or the hardware itself is malfunctioning – while a red cross means the hardware is disabled.

If you see an exclamation mark next to your sound card, you'll need to reinstall the driver. This should be included on a disc that came with your computer, but if you don't have one, you'll need to download the drivers. Most PCs and all laptops have built-in sound cards, which means it's fairly easy to identify the make and model. For PCs, you can either search on the manufacturer's website or the motherboard manufacturer's site. For laptops, it's usually best to visit the manufacturer's website. You can recognise a built-in sound card by the fact that its ports are located with others on the rear of your PC, rather than on a separate card adjacent to the main ports.

If you see a red cross, you can try re-enabling the hardware by right-clicking on it and choosing Enable. You may still need to install the drivers after doing this.

CHECK THE BIOS

You may find that there are no sound devices listed in Device Manager. In this case, you should reboot your computer and enter the BIOS (for more on this, see Chapter 5 on page 78). In the BIOS, look for a menu titled Integrated peripherals, and scan the list for AC'97 or HD Audio. If it's disabled, you simply need to enable it, save the changes and exit the BIOS. When you reboot, Windows should detect new hardware and either install drivers automatically or prompt you to locate them.

If the sound card is enabled in the BIOS but doesn't show up in Device Manager, the hardware is probably faulty and you'll need a new sound card. The easiest option is to buy a USB sound card, as this won't require you to open up your PC. This is your only option if you have a laptop. If you don't mind opening your PC, you can buy a PCI sound card or, if you have a modern motherboard with PCI Express slots, a PCI-E 1x sound card.

↑ Make sure that the correct playback device is set as the default option

↑ Playback and Recording devices are displayed on separate tabs in the Sound section

Solving monitor problems

AS WITH THE other peripherals covered in this chapter, monitor problems may or may not be fixable. Here we'll address a few common problems that you can solve without calling your display manufacturer.

The most obvious problem is that there's no image on the screen. You need to find out if the fault lies with your PC or your monitor. As we've already shown in Chapter 2, there are several reasons why your PC may refuse to boot, and some of them could cause the screen to be blank.

It's worth checking the basics first. Ensure that the power and signal cables are firmly attached to the monitor, as well as to the wall socket and the PC. If your monitor is plugged into a power strip, make sure that both the wall switch and any switches on the power strip are turned on.

Most monitors, whether CRT or LCD, show a warning message if no input signal is detected. If you see such a message, it's clear that the display is working. Some monitors have multiple inputs, so you need to select the appropriate one to view the incoming signal. There should be a dedicated button on the monitor for this, but it may be hidden in the onscreen menus.

If you do see a Windows screen but it's showing incorrect colours, disconnect and reconnect the video cable at both ends and tighten it securely. A loose cable is a common cause of

↑LCD screens can warn you if there's no signal or if a signal is out of range

colour corruption. If you're using a VGA cable with an LCD screen and you see fuzzy text or the entire Windows desktop is shifted off one edge, use your monitor's Auto setting to re-sync the signal. If this doesn't work, try using the manual clock and phase options in the monitor's menu system.

Another common LCD problem is stuck pixels, where a dot constantly shows one colour (red, green, blue, white or black) irrespective of what Windows is showing. If this is the case, it's worth trying a free utility such as UDPixel from *http://udpix.free.fr* to see if it can be changed. Such applications rapidly change the colours onscreen for several hours in an effort to coax the pixel into life. UDPixel is helpful as it can show the five possible colours across the whole screen to help you identify where any defective pixels are located.

On older CRT monitors, you may see dark patches in the corners or at the edges of the screen. It's often possible to correct these by using the monitor's degauss function in the menus. If this doesn't work, move any magnetic sources such as unshielded speakers away from the monitor.

A GUIDE TO INTERFACES
VGA

VGA (also known as D-sub) has been a standard PC video connection since 1987, and is the most basic PC graphics connection. The VGA connector supports resolutions of up to 2,048x1,536. VGA connectors carry an analogue signal made up of

↓ Dead or stuck pixels may be fixable using a utility such as the free UDPixel

UndeadPixel 2.2	— □ X
Dead pixel locator	**Undead pixel**
Red	Flash windows : 1
Lime	Flash size : 5X5
Blue	Flash interval : (25 ms)
White	
Black	
Yellow ...	Start Reset
Run cycle 1	Choose number and size of flashing area plus flash time interval. Then press start and move flashing area into your dead pixels.
Press each button and locate your dead pixel.	
Our website : UDPixel	
Any suggestion, please send mail to : udpixel@gmail.com	
Does it work ? ... so encourage people who make free software for you, make a gift : PayPal DONATE	

the component colours – red, green and blue – as well as horizontal and vertical timing data.

VGA was designed for CRT monitors, which required this timing data to draw the picture using an electron gun firing in a series of lines at phosphors on the screen. LCD monitors paint the same picture using different voltages applied to rows of pixels, so they need to convert this timing data. This is done automatically and rarely causes problems, but for fine control you should look for Pixel Clock and Phase settings on your monitor's onscreen display menu. Test patterns are available on the web to help you set these up correctly.

DVI

The next step up from VGA is DVI, which supports a maximum resolution of 2,560x1,600 (the highest any consumer connection can currently offer) and can carry both analogue and digital signals. Most modern video cards have two DVI outputs. One of the most practical advantages of using a monitor with a DVI input rather than a VGA connection is that you don't need to fiddle with timing data, because in its native resolution a DVI output transmits data for each pixel on an LCD screen.

There are five main types of DVI connection (see the picture on the right), which makes it a bit more confusing than other connectors. DVI-A (Analogue) supports only analogue signals, and has the fewest pins on its connector. DVI-D (Digital) is a digital-only version found on most modern LCD monitors, and can be distinguished by the narrower flat pin, which doesn't include four pins arranged in a square around it.

DVI-I (Integrated) allows for both analogue and digital signals, and is standard on most modern video cards. DVI-I has a wider flat pin, plus the four analogue signal pins. This means that a male DVI-D connector can fit into a female DVI-I port,

↘ There are several types of DVI cable

allowing you to connect your digital monitor to your PC; you can also connect a DVI-to-VGA adaptor to this port or DVI-A cable, so you can plug in analogue monitors. A male DVI-I connector won't fit into the narrower flat pin on a DVI-D female port, so you can't connect incompatible devices.

To make things more confusing, there are also dual-link versions of DVI-I and DVI-D. These support higher bandwidth connections for displays over 1,920x1,200, such as huge 30in models, which can support resolutions of up to 2,560x1,600. Dual-link connectors can be distinguished by the six extra pins in the middle of the two banks of nine pins. To use dual-link, you'll also need a graphics card with a dual-link output.

HDMI

DVI has a few limitations compared to the newest standard, HDMI. As well having a standard connector to make things simpler, HDMI also carries high-definition audio and remote control signals. This means you can reduce the number of wires connected between your monitor, speakers and PC. The remote control features allow devices made by the same manufacturer to communicate with each other, so you can set timers to record TV programmes, for example.

HDMI also supports High-bandwidth Digital Content Protection (HDCP) encryption as standard. This is a copy-protection system that is standard on multimedia devices such as Blu-ray players, and you won't be able to watch copy-protected films without it. HDMI is backwards-compatible with DVI, so with the right adaptors, you can connect from a DVI port on your PC to an HDMI-equipped monitor, and vice versa. HDCP is not always enabled on DVI ports, however, so it's worth checking that both your PC and your monitor will support it.

DISPLAYPORT

The final type of connector is DisplayPort, a new digital connector that supports resolutions up to 3,840x2,160 over a single cable. This input is available on only a few current monitors, but it is becoming increasingly common on a number of graphics cards.

DisplayPort isn't compatible with HDMI or DVI, although the DisplayPort connector can pass both of these signals through. This allows graphics card manufacturers to create products that are compatible with DisplayPort and DVI monitors.

DVI-I (single link)

DVI-I (dual link)

DVI-D (single link)

DVI-D (dual link)

DVI-A

Testing memory

MEMORY IS ONE of the most important components in your PC. It stores every aspect of the programs and data that you're currently running, from the window showing your holiday snaps to the spreadsheet with your accounts. Memory also holds important Windows data, such as device driver information and the core components of how Windows works.

A problem with memory can, therefore, be incredibly serious. For example, if your memory should corrupt a critical part of Windows, when the processor tries to use this data it can end up causing a serious system crash. This can result in damage to Windows and the loss of important data that you may have been working on.

To prevent this happening, it's worth running some diagnostic tests on your computer using the free Memtest86+ (*www.memtest.org*). This utility runs directly from a bootable CD before Windows has started and performs a series of tests on your system memory. Any problems reported here could lead to major problems in Windows. The step-by-step guide opposite shows you how to run the test, but here we'll explain what to do with the results.

ERRORS

An error doesn't automatically mean that you have a major problem with your memory. First, try checking the BIOS to find out what speed your memory is running at (see page 78 for instructions on how to do this). If it's running faster than it's supposed to, then you could be pushing it too much. Our guide on testing for system heat on page 154 is also worth checking. If your system's temperature is too high, then your PC could be suffering from its effects.

It's always worth checking the obvious things, too. If you didn't plug your memory all the way in, it may be detected but cause intermittent faults. Try unplugging your memory and reseating it. Once you've done this try, run the Memtest86+ program again to see if the problem has disappeared. If it hasn't, it's time to try a new tack.

SWITCH SLOTS

It could be that one of the memory slots is causing the problem. Try switching memory slots on your motherboard and rerunning the test. If you're getting the same error, there's probably something wrong with your memory. You can attempt to find out which stick of RAM is causing the problems by taking out all the memory bar one stick and running the tests again. By rotating the stick of installed memory, you'll be able to track down the offending module.

As processors access memory through their own onboard caches, your processor could be causing the error. If you change your memory and the problem persists, you should change the processor or motherboard.

HOW TO...
Test your memory

1 CREATE BOOT DISC

Memtest86+ runs from a CD. Download the ISO file from *www.memtest.org* and save it to your hard disk. If you already have a CD-burning utility such as CDBurnerXP, you can follow the instructions for writing the ISO file to CD. If you haven't, download the free ISO Recorder from *http://isorecorder.alexfeinman.com*. Version 2 is for Windows XP and Version 3 is for Vista and Windows 7, so make sure you get the right one.

Once the software's installed, find the ISO file you downloaded, right-click on it and select Copy image to CD. Put a blank disc in your optical drive and click Next.

2 BOOT FROM THE CD

Put the CD that you just created into your drive and restart the computer. Make sure that your BIOS is set to boot from the optical drive. The CD will automatically load the test environment and start running the tests.

On the screen, you'll see system information and the current test status. The test can take 20 minutes or more to run, so you should leave it running. When it finishes, you'll either get details of

the errors discovered or a message saying that your memory has passed the test.

3 COMPARE DATA

The details on the screen show you the speed at which your memory is running. This is displayed after the settings heading, in brackets after DDR. You should compare this to the speed at which it's supposed to be running. If the detected speed is faster than the memory's rated speed, you could have a problem. However, don't worry about small fluctuations in speed, such as a difference of around five per cent. It's common for the timings to be slightly wrong and components made to run a bit quicker than their rated speeds.

4 CONFIGURE TEST

If you want to configure which test to run, you need to press C while the initial test is running. You may need to reset your computer and boot from the CD you created to get this option. In the menu, press 1 to access the test selection. Press 3 to select the test you want to run, and then type a number from 0 to 9 to run that test. You can find a list of the tests on the Memtest website.

TIP

Often, only one stick of memory is at fault, so it's worth replacing each stick one by one to try and solve any problems.

Testing your hard disk

WE'VE ALL BECOME used to having masses of storage space, which most of us stuff full of gigabytes of photos, videos, music and important documents without a second thought. As wonderful as this all is, hard disks are mechanical and therefore quite sensitive. They can fail rapidly and, even if they don't lock up completely, they can cause problems with some files.

Although you should make regular backups of your data, it's also worth checking your hard disk if you're suffering from problems to make sure that it's working properly. Don't worry if you encounter a problem, as you can use third-party software such as Acronis True Image (*www.acronis.co.uk*) to take an image of your PC and restore this to a new hard disk.

We'll show you how to test your hard disk for free using Hitachi GST's Drive Fitness Test application (*www.hitachigst.com/hdd/support/download.htm*). Although it's made by Hitachi, it works on all brands of hard disks. It's run from a bootable CD, which we'll show you how to make.

HOW HARD DISKS WORK

The problem with hard disks is that they're mechanical, and are therefore prone to faults. Inside the sealed enclosure are a series of platters, which are disks stacked above each other. These platters, like floppy disks, store data magnetically, and are written to and read by heads that sit just above the surface. Hard disks are therefore very sensitive to movements, as sudden jerks can make the heads touch the platter and destroy any data that's stored on the disk.

If you get problems when you run Drive Fitness Test, make sure your hard disk is firmly attached inside the case and that your computer is standing on a level surface. We've known of a computer that was kept on an old wobbly desk constantly having problems with corrupted Windows files.

PROBLEM DETECTION

Other problems can affect a disk, including lots of bad areas on the disk (known as sectors). These might be detected in normal use only when you fill your disk up and your computer starts trying to access these areas. By running a system scan beforehand, you can detect these bad sectors

now. These will be marked as bad by the hard disk, which prevents data being written to them, but you should replace the hard disk if you find that you get a large number of bad sectors.

Mechanical problems are also a big worry. A damaged disk can make a horrible, metallic clunking sound. While there's little that can be done to prevent this in the long term, running diagnostic tests that access the whole disk can warn you of potential mechanical failure in the future by giving the hard disk a good workout.

Heat, as for other components, can cause massive problems inside a hard disk, so make sure that the inside of your PC is kept cool, and add more cooling if necessary (see page 154 for more information).

Modern hard disks have built-in S.M.A.R.T. technology. This lets your BIOS and other applications talk to the disk and see if there are any problems. S.M.A.R.T. can also notify you of an impending disk failure before it happens.

Finally, the interface between the hard disk and your PC can cause problems if it's damaged. In this case, there's nothing you can do but replace the hard disk. It's worth checking that the cables are plugged in firmly first, though.

HOW TO...
Test your hard disk

1 CREATE BOOT DISC

Drive Fitness Test runs from a CD that you can create yourself. Download the ISO file from *www.hitachigst.com/hdd/support/download.htm* and save it to your hard disk. If you already have a CD-burning utility, you can use that to write the ISO file to CD.

If you don't have a CD-burning application, download the free ISO Recorder from *http://isorecorder.alexfeinman.com*. Version 2 is for Windows XP and Version 3 is for Vista and Windows 7, so make sure you get the right one. Once the it's installed, right-click on the ISO file and select Copy image to CD. Put a blank CD into your optical drive and click Next.

2 BOOT FROM THE CD

Put the CD in your optical drive and restart your PC. Set the BIOS so that your optical drive is the first boot device (see page 78). You'll be given a menu with a choice of two options. Select the second option, press Enter and accept the licence agreement. The Drive Fitness Test program will then detect your hard disks, and ask for confirmation that this list is correct. Select Yes.

3 RUN A QUICK TEST

Select the hard disk that you want to test and then choose Quick Test. On the next screen, click Start. Drive Fitness Test will now run a series of diagnostic tests on your hard disk to make sure it's working properly. If the software detects any errors, you'll be told at the end of the test; otherwise, you'll get a green completion message. Click OK to accept it.

With a brand new disk this should be good enough to show that it's working correctly. If you're testing a hard disk from an old computer, follow Step 4 for a more in-depth test.

4 ADVANCED TEST

The Quick Test doesn't give the drive a full workout. For this you need to run the Advanced Test. This will run more thorough tests and check the surface of the disk for errors.

As this involves checking every part of the disk, this test will take a lot longer to run than the Quick Test, but it's worth doing, particularly if you're checking an old hard disk. It's also essential if you think that your hard disk could be causing problems.

TIP
You should run Windows Check Disk on your hard disks regularly to find and fix faults before they become too serious.

Testing your new PC for heat

EVERYTHING INSIDE YOUR computer generates heat to some degree. It may seem obvious that your processor does – after all, it has a giant fan and heatsink on top of it – but all components produce a certain amount of heat. Memory, hard disks, graphics cards and even your optical drive all contribute to the overall internal temperature of your PC's case.

Heat is a big problem inside computers. If your PC is too hot, you'll find that it will crash more often, as the components shut themselves down to prevent damage. In the long term, the effects of too much heat inside your system can cause your components to have a shorter lifespan. In the case of your hard disk, this could see it failing before its time, taking some of your important data with it.

MONITOR AND MEASURE

It's really important, therefore, to make sure that your PC is running at the right temperature. Keeping it cool will save you trouble and hassle further down the line. Our step-by-step guide on the opposite page shows you how to monitor your computer's temperature with the free utility SpeedFan. You can download this from *www. almico.com/speedfan.php*.

Click the download tab and click the link in the download section of the page. Once installed, it can monitor and help control the temperature inside your PC. Before you can set it properly, though, you need to know what should be expected from your system.

IDEAL TEMPERATURES

To get SpeedFan working properly, you'll have to set some maximum temperatures. These can be tricky to work out, but we've got some tips that should help. Hard disks, for example, shouldn't run any higher than 55°C, or they can be damaged. Overall system temperature inside the case should be kept below 50°C, but the lower the better.

Processors are harder to measure, as it depends on the type of chip that you're using. Generally speaking, AMD processors should have an external temperature of less than 40°C. Intel processors should have an external temperature of less than 55°C.

You may find that, depending on your system, your temperatures are either close to these figures or a lot lower. Much depends on the temperature sensors in your PC. Motherboard manufacturers use different types of sensors in different locations, which can cause a lot of variance between boards. As long as you're running your PC at temperatures less than we've highlighted, though, it will be fine.

MORE FANS

If your PC is running really hot, there are some things you can try to lower the temperature. First, reseat your processor cooler, making sure it has enough thermal paste on it to increase the efficiency of the heatsink. Make sure your case's fans aren't clogged up with dust. If you can control your fans manually, try turning them up.

Finally, if you haven't got any case fans or have enough space for more, then install some. They're easy to fit, and pretty much every case has mountings for them. Inspect your case's manual for full instructions on the size of fans you can install. Ideally, you want to get airflow moving through the case to extract hot air. So, if your fan at the rear is blowing out the back of the case, fit one in the front that blows into the case. This will bring in cool air from outside and help push the hot air out of the case. If you have one hot component, such as a hard disk, then you need to fit fans near it to help cool it down.

HOW TO...
Monitor system temperature

1 READINGS

SpeedFan automatically detects temperature sensors on the motherboard and displays their current readings. Unfortunately, it doesn't always give them recognisable names, so it can be hard to tell which one is your processor's temperature and which one is the system temperature. The easiest way to find out is to leave your system idle for a few minutes until the temperatures settle. Note down the temperatures, restart your computer and go into the BIOS. Its monitoring section will give you real names for the sensors – all you have to do is match the relative values you recorded.

SpeedFan places an icon next to each temperature reading, which is designed to show you the current status of your computer. A green tick means that everything's all right, arrows show whether the temperature is increasing or decreasing, while a fire means that it's too hot. However, SpeedFan doesn't always get the warnings right, so ignore them for now.

2 HDD AND CORE

As well as accessing the motherboard, SpeedFan can read the temperature of your hard disks using Self-Monitoring Analysis and Reporting Technology (S.M.A.R.T.). Each disk in your PC will be numbered (HD0, HD1 and so on) and have its own temperature. You can also get a report on

your hard disk by clicking on the S.M.A.R.T. tab. The core temperatures are the readings from inside your processor.

3 CONFIGURE SETTINGS

Click on the Readings tab and then on Configure. You'll see the list of temperature sensors. Click to select one, wait a few seconds and then click again. You can now rename the sensor to match what you identified in Step 1. Press Enter to set the name.

Click on a sensor and you'll see two readings: desired and warning. The first is an ideal temperature, while warning determines when a flame will be displayed. You only need to set the warning temperatures for hard disks and the processor, as defined by the limits opposite.

4 CHARTS

Click on the Charts tab and put ticks in the sensors that you want to measure. SpeedFan will then track temperatures over time. This is a good way to see how your system responds when you do different jobs. For example, if you play a lot of games and see that your PC's temperature is running very high during this activity, you'll know that you need to get some extra cooling. This can also be useful when running burn-in tests, such as Hot CPU Tester (see page 156).

TIP
Fans have arrows printed on them showing the direction of the airflow.

Testing your processor

THE PROCESSOR IS just about the most important part of your PC. Without it, you'd just have a collection of components that wouldn't be able to do anything. The processor controls every single aspect of your computer, from loading and running the operating system to running the clever artificial intelligence in the latest games.

Processors are constantly being updated, and are also becoming more complicated. These days, it's the norm for a single chip to house at least two processors (called cores), but four cores are rapidly becoming more affordable. While this extra complexity means that computers today can storm through tough tasks such as video encoding quicker than ever, the result is that there's more that can go wrong.

A processor crashing will immediately freeze your computer, losing any unsaved work in the process. If the hard disk was being accessed at the time with an important Windows system file

open, a processor crash can even mean that you need to reinstall Windows. Here we'll show you how to test your computer for stability with the free Hot CPU Tester (available from *www.7byte.com*).

PROBLEM SOLVING

The free version of Hot CPU Tester doesn't run the full suite of diagnostics, which is available in the Professional version. However, there's enough there to make sure that your processor is running properly. Using its Burn-in test, you can find out how effective your processor's cooling is.

The most common reason for a processor to fail any of the diagnostic tests is overheating. Processors are sensitive to heat, and can start causing errors when they get too hot. Intel's processors try to deal with the problem by slowing themselves down, which makes your computer very sluggish until the core temperature has dropped. Alternatively, processors can shut themselves down completely, meaning that you'll need to restart your computer.

COOLING OFF

The essential thing with processors is to make sure that there's plenty of cooling. Follow our step-by-step advice opposite to work out how hot your processor is. If it exceeds the limits we set on page 154, you've got a problem. Take your PC apart and make sure that its fan is working and that there's decent contact between the processor and the cooler. You may need to reapply thermal paste.

If heat doesn't seem to be the problem and your processor is still failing diagnostic checks, make sure you're running it at the intended speed in the BIOS (see page 78). Running the processor faster than it is meant to can cause errors.

Finally, try taking the processor out of its socket (see pages 56 and 57 for full instructions). In Intel LGA-775 sockets, look for any bent pins. If you see any, push them gently back into place with a jeweller's screwdriver. For AM2 and AM2+ processors, make sure that you haven't bent any pins on the processor. Inserting a credit card between the rows should allow you to bend them back into shape. Take great care when doing this or you could cause more damage.

HOW TO...
Test your processor

1 SET THE TEST DURATION

Install Hot CPU Tester (*www.7byte.com*) and run it when the installation has finished. Click OK to skip the message about upgrading to the new version. Before you start, click on the Options tab and select the Test Modules item. You'll see that the test duration is set to six hours. While this will give your PC a thorough workout, it's probably too much for most people. We'd recommend setting it to an hour or slightly under.

2 RUN TEST

Click on the Diagnostic button and click Run Test. Hot CPU Tester will then give your processor a thorough workout. It will run lots of mathematically complex tasks to stretch your processor to its limit. It will use every core in your PC, so you'll be unable to use your computer for anything else during this time.

Once the program has finished the test, you'll receive a report telling you if your processor failed any of the tests. If it didn't, you know that it's working properly.

3 BURN IN

Click the Burn-in icon. This test will run your processor at 100 per cent load, and is useful for checking how temperature affects it. However, in the free version of Hot CPU Tester, which tests only a single core, you can run only a single thread. A workaround is to run Hot CPU Tester as many times as you have cores by double-clicking the program icon.

4 MEASURE

Before you start the Burn-in test, run SpeedFan (see page 155) in order to measure the temperature. Keep it somewhere onscreen where it will be visible. Start the Burn-in test on every open copy of Hot CPU Tester by clicking the Run CPU Burn-in button. SpeedFan may stop responding, as your processor is too busy to deal with it. Don't worry; just leave the test running for around 10 minutes and then stop all the Burn-in tests. When they've stopped, look at the temperature of the processor in SpeedFan. If it's exceeded the limits you set for it, you may have overheating problems.

TIP
If you have fan speed switches on or inside your case, try using them to increase fan speed to cool down a hot processor.

Glossary

Cut through the jargon with our plain English guide

10/100Mbit/s See Ethernet.

10BASE-T See Ethernet.

64-BIT 64-bit processors have an extended instruction set, allowing them to process more data at once and access more memory. Only software that supports 64-bit extensions will benefit.

802.11n See WiFi.

ADSL Asymmetric digital subscriber line, the commonest form of broadband. It works over existing BT phone lines, provided that the local exchange is ADSL-enabled.

AGP Accelerated graphics port, a slot for graphics cards. Several versions of increasing speed and decreasing voltage were launched. Now superseded by PCI Express.

ATA AT attachment. See IDE.

ATAPI AT attachment packet interface. See IDE.

ATHLON 64 AMD's old mainstream processor, which was available in single- and dual-core (X2) versions.

ATHLON X2 Dual-core processor based on the Phenom's design and compatible with AM2 and AM3 motherboards.

ATX POWER CONNECTOR This PSU connector supplies the PC's motherboard. It was previously a 20-pin connector, but a 24-pin version started appearing on motherboards in 2005. A split connector is commonly provided to power either version.

ATX See Form Factor.

BIOS Basic input/output system; configures your motherboard at startup and boots your PC. It's stored on a flash memory chip and keeps its settings in the CMOS.

BLANKING PLATE Used to cover unoccupied PC case cutouts. You must remove one to install a PCI, PCI Express or AGP expansion card.

BTX See Form Factor.

CARDBUS The 32-bit expansion slot most commonly found on laptop PCs, equivalent to the PCI slot on desktops. Now being superseded by ExpressCard.

CAT5, CAT6 See Ethernet.

CELERON DUAL-CORE Budget dual-core processor which is based on the Core 2 Duo and compatible with LGA775 motherboards.

CLOCK SPEED All computer components work in time with a clock signal. Each has a maximum speed, shown in megahertz (MHz) or gigahertz (GHz), at which it's designed to run. Running the clock faster (overclocking) boosts performance, but can cause a PC to crash.

CMOS Battery-backed memory where the BIOS stores its settings. Can be cleared using a jumper.

COMPONENT VIDEO A high-quality analogue video connection that uses three cables to connect to your devices.

COMPOSITE VIDEO A basic-quality video connection using a single cable.

CORE 2 Intel's most common processor, available for LGA775 in mainstream Duo and Quad and premium Extreme versions.

CORE i3, i5, i7 Intel's latest processors have a completely new architecture and work in LGA1366 or LGA1156 motherboards.

CPU Central processing unit, also known simply as a processor.

CROSSFIRE ATI's system for combining the power of two Radeon graphics cards in a single PC. Also see SLI.

CRT Cathode ray tube. A conventional glass-tube monitor.

DDR The type of memory used in many PCs, called double data rate because it runs twice as fast as its clock speed. Comes in several speeds, including PC2700 and PC3200. PC3200 DDR runs at 200MHz but is called 400MHz DDR because of its doubled effective speed.

DDR2 The type of memory used in the majority of Pentium 4, Core 2, Athlon 64 and Phenom systems. Available in speeds from PC2-4200 (533MHz effective).

DDR3 The type of memory used by all new processors. It's available in speeds from PC3-6400 (800MHz), up to PC3-12800 (1,600MHz).

DHCP Dynamic host configuration protocol. This allows PCs on a network to obtain their network configuration automatically from a DHCP server.

DIRECTX Windows extensions from Microsoft that give games and other performance-hungry software fast access to hardware. Check that your PC has the latest version – currently DirectX 10 – installed.

D-SUB Analogue monitor-to-graphics-card connection, also known as a VGA cable.

DUAL-CHANNEL Refers to the capability of a processor or motherboard to access two DIMMs at once, thus improving system performance.

DVB-T Digital Video Broadcasting – Terrestrial, a standard used by Freeview digital TV in the UK.

DVI Digital visual interface. A monitor-to-graphics-card connection that can include digital and/or analogue signals. The commonest form, DVI-I, has both.

ETHERNET Non-specific networking term, today used to refer to any networking hardware using RJ45 plugs and one of a number of compatible standards including 10BaseT, 100BaseT and Gigabit Ethernet (GbE). Older 10/100Mbit/s hardware supports the two slower speeds, and runs reliably with the Category 5 (Cat5) grade of cable. Cat5e cables are needed for Gigabit Ethernet.

EXPRESSCARD Expansion slot found on new laptop PCs, equivalent to PCI Express on desktops. Incompatible with CardBus.

FAT32 See NTFS.

FIREWALL Software or hardware designed to protect networks from hackers or from software that they control.

FIREWIRE Also known as IEEE 1394 or i.Link. Fast data connection used by PCs, digital camcorders, external hard disks and more. The connector comes in four-pin and six-pin versions, the latter including pins to power one device from the other. A faster nine-pin version, known as FireWire 800, is backward-compatible.

FIRMWARE Software used by a hardware device and stored on a flash memory chip so that it can be upgraded, typically to improve compatibility.

FLASH A type of memory chip that stores data permanently unless it is deliberately overwritten, a process known as flashing.

FLOPPY POWER CONNECTOR
A compact four-pin power connector for floppy drives.

FORM FACTOR Motherboards adhere to standards called form factors that dictate size and layout. The commonest are ATX and its compact relative microATX. BTX is Intel's newest standard. Cases will support one or more form factors, telling you which motherboards can be fitted.

FSB Frontside bus. This connects the processor and other parts of the system in older Intel systems.

GIGABIT ETHERNET (GbE) See Ethernet.

HEADER A group of pins on a motherboard where you can connect additional ports. USB and FireWire headers are the most common.

HYPERTRANSPORT AMD's proprietary bus, which allows the processor to talk directly to other system components.

IDE A common name for the ATA disk connector, strictly called ATAPI in its modern form, which supports a variety of devices. All three are also known as PATA (Parallel ATA), to distinguish them from SATA (Serial ATA).

IEEE 1394 See FireWire.

JUMPER A plastic-enclosed metal contact which is used to connect two pins to configure a hardware device; for example, see Master.

LGA775 Intel's current processor socket, which has pins rather than holes. LGA775 is used by Pentium 4, Celeron and Core 2 processors.

LGA1366 Intel's current processor socket. An update to LGA775, designed for use with the Core i7 range of processors.

LINE-IN Audio input for signal of standard 'line-level' volume (louder than microphone input). Usually light blue and takes a 3.5mm jack.

LINE-OUT Audio output of standard 'line-level' volume. Usually lime green, and takes a 3.5mm jack.

LLANO AMD's latest processor type. It has built-in graphics, giving you gaming performance with low power consumption.

MASTER Two IDE devices can share a single cable, provided that one is configured as a master and the other as a slave. This is done using jumpers on the devices.

MICROATX A compact mainstream motherboard form factor with a maximum size of 244x244mm.

MINI CARD Generic term for a laptop's internal expansion cards.

MOLEX Common name for the four-pin power connector used by hard disks and other drives. It has yellow (12V), red (5V) and two black (ground) wires.

NTFS Hard disk file system used by XP, Vista, 7 and other advanced versions of Windows. Replaces FAT32, as used by Windows 95, 98 and Me.

OEM Original equipment manufacturer. Used to describe products intended for PC manufacturers rather than end users. Typically these will have minimal packaging and manuals.

PATA See IDE.

PCI A motherboard expansion slot used for all kinds of upgrade cards except graphics cards. Internal modems, TV tuners and sound cards generally use PCI.

PCI EXPRESS (PCI-E) New expansion bus for all kinds of upgrades. Slots come in several lengths. Long, fast x16 slots are for graphics cards; short, slower x1 slots are for devices previously made for PCI. A slower card can be used in a faster slot.

PENTIUM 4 Intel's old range of processors, now obsolete.

PENTIUM DUAL-CORE Dual-core processors based on the Core 2 Duo design and designed for use in LGA775 motherboards.

PHENOM AMD's processor is designed for Socket AM2+ and AM3 motherboards, but can work with some older Socket AM2 boards, too. Comes in quad-core (X4) and tri-core (X3) versions. Black Editions can be overclocked easily.

PHENOM II An update to the Phenom, also designed for use with Socket AM2+ and AM3 motherboards, but can work with some older Socket AM2 boards, too. Comes in dual-core (X2), tri-core (X3) and quad-core (X4) versions. Black Editions can be overclocked easily.

PHONO Hi-fi style interconnect, correctly known as an RCA jack and used for various audio and video connections. Red and white plugs are used for right and left audio channels, yellow for composite video.

POST Power-on self-test, performed by PCs when switched on, generating the text output that you see before Windows loads. Error messages are often displayed here, too.

PRIMARY CHANNEL Most motherboards provide at least two IDE connectors for hard disks and other drives. The PC will boot from the master disk on the connector marked as the primary channel. The secondary channel is typically used for CD and DVD drives.

PS/2 CONNECTOR Used for keyboards and mice, although these now often connect via USB.

PSU Power supply unit. Refers to the device inside a PC that converts mains electricity and distributes it to the system's components, and also to the external mains adaptors supplied with some peripherals.

QUICKPATH INTERCONNECT Intel's proprietary bus, which lets the processor talk directly to other system components.

RAID Redundant array of inexpensive disks: a way of storing data on several hard disks to improve performance, or to provide a backup if one disk fails, or both.

RF Radio frequency, referring to the coaxial cable connection of TV antennas. An RF signal carries many video channels, while S-video and composite carry only one.

RJ45 The plug used for Ethernet network cables, with eight wires. Larger than, but often mistaken for, RJ11.

SATA The Serial ATA interface is used for modern hard disks because it's faster and neater than PATA (Parallel ATA). The original SATA ran at 150MB/s, but the current standard has a 300MB/s mode, compared to PATA's maximum of 133MB/s.

SDRAM The memory type used by most Pentium II and Pentium III PCs.

SECONDARY CHANNEL See Primary Channel.

SERIAL PORT Old, slow port rarely used today but still present on some motherboards as a nine-pin connector.

SLAVE See Master.

SLI Nvidia's system for combining the power of two GeForce graphics cards in one PC. Also see CrossFire.

SOCKET 478 Intel's previous-generation processor socket, used by Intel's old Pentium 4 and Celeron processors.

SOCKET M Socket for Intel's original mobile Core and Core 2 Duo Mobile processors. It has since been replaced with the newer Socket P.

SOCKET P Socket used by Intel's latest Core 2 mobile processors. It has the same number of pins as Socket M, but isn't backwards-compatible.

SOCKET 939 Socket used by AMD's Athlon 64 processors, including dual-core X2 versions. Supports processors with a dual memory controller.

SOCKET AM2 AMD's processor socket, which supports DDR2 memory. Used by Athlon 64, Athlon FX and Sempron processors. This has now been replaced.

SOCKET AM2+ A newer AMD processor socket, which supports PC-8500 DDR2 memory and the Phenom range of processors. Backwards-compatible with older processors.

SOCKET AM3 AMD's processor socket, which supports DDR3 memory and Phenom II processors. This socket is not backwards-compatible with older AM2 or AM2+ processors.

SOCKET FM1 AMD's latest processor socket, which supports Llano processors.

SSD Solid state drive: a hard disk replacement that uses flash memory for improved speed and performance.

S-VIDEO An average-quality analogue video connection with a four-pin cable.

TV-OUT Generic analogue output used for connection to a TV. Includes S-video and composite.

USB Universal serial bus. These ports are used to connect all manner of external devices. USB2 is the most common, but faster USB3 is also available.

VIVO Video in, video out. A connector on graphics cards that combines video inputs and outputs. Usually has a breakout cable that maps the pins to standard S-video, component or composite video connectors.

WEP Wired equivalent privacy. An encryption standard used to secure wireless networks. It's insecure and should not be used.

WIFI Name used collectively for the IEEE 802.11 wireless networking standards, including the 300Mbit/s 802.11n standard.

WPA WiFi protected access. An encryption standard used to secure wireless networks more reliably than WEP. WPA2 is the latest standard and should be used where supported.

BUILD A BETTER PC 2012

EDITORIAL

Editor
David Ludlow

Production
Steve Haines

Design and layout
Colin Mackleworth

COVER ILLUSTRATION
Ian Naylor

PHOTOGRAPHY
Danny Bird
Jan Cihak
Linda Duong
Pat Hall
Timo Hebditch
Andrew Ridge
Hugh Threlfall

MANAGEMENT

MagBooks Manager
Dharmesh Mistry

Digital Production Manager
Nicky Baker

Managing Director
John Garewal

Managing Director of Advertising
Julian Lloyd-Evans

Newstrade Director
David Barker

Chief Operating Officer
Brett Reynolds

Group Finance Director
Ian Leggett

Chief Executive
James Tye

Chairman
Felix Dennis

 MAGBOOK

MAGBOOK
The 'MagBook' brand is a trademark of Dennis Publishing Ltd, 30 Cleveland St, London W1T 4JD. Company registered in England. All material © Dennis Publishing Ltd, licensed by Felden 2011, and may not be reproduced in whole or part without the consent of the publishers.

LICENSING & SYNDICATION
To license this product, please contact Hannah Heagney, hannah_heagney@ dennis.co.uk, +44 20 7907 6134.
For syndication queries, please contact Anj Dosaj-Halai, anj_dosaj-halai@dennis. co.uk, +44 20 7907 6132.

LIABILITY
While every care was taken during the production of this MagBook, the publishers cannot be held responsible for the accuracy of the information or any consequence arising from it. Dennis Publishing takes no responsibility for the companies advertising in this MagBook.

The paper used within this MagBook is produced from sustainable fibre, manufactured by mills with a valid chain of custody.

Printed by BGP

ISBN 1-907779-44-2

♻ **recycle**
When you have finished with this magazine please recycle it.